SIMULATION SECRETS

Don't Be Afraid

CASPER STITH

Beforehand

Please approach this information skeptically and with an open-minded curiosity.

Deep-seated beliefs and biases often cause us to think that we have it all figured out. The following information will likely challenge many of those beliefs.

Please accept nothing as fact and independently research and validate any and all information contained herein.

We live in a virtual reality – and **things will never be the same.**

Please come along for the ride, while leaving your baggage at the door, for it can always be retrieved on the way out.

"All truth passes through three stages. First, it is ridiculed. Second, it is violently opposed. Third, it is accepted as being self-evident." - Arthur Schopenhauer (1788-1860)

Table of Contents

Virtual Reality 1

  'The Sims' 2

Simulation Prognostication 3

'Science' 6

Weird Science 9

  Heisenberg 11

  Tunneling 13

    'The Wave' 15

  Quantum Entanglement.................................. 17

  To Kill a Cat 19

  The Double-Slit Experiment 21

    Delayed Choice 26

  Let's Get Digital 29

    'It from Bit'...31

'The One' 33

'The End of Science' 35

'My Big Toe' 38

  'The Larger Consciousness System' 41

    Consciousness – 'The Hard Problem'.................44

    The 'Great Machine' 48

  Free Will.. 52

  Entropy 55

  A Chip off the Old Block 59

  Free Will Awareness Units 62

Reality Frames **63**

   Near-Death Experiences 65

   Remote Viewing 68

This Virtual Life: Simulation Specifications **71**

   Self-organization 72

   The Code.. 73

   Fractals 78

   Order from Chaos 82

   The *Quantum* Computer 86

   The Rules 90

   Probability Distribution 95

   Psi Uncertainty 97

The Game **99**

   The Nash Equilibrium 103

The Player **106**

   Self.. 109

   Beliefs 110

   Ego.. 112

   Fear... 117

Choices **121**

The Objective **123**

   Self-Destruction.. 128

The Secret **132**

   The Placebo Effect 135

   Operation Entropy-Reduction 139

The Database **160**

'Experience Packets' **163**

Simulation Speculation ***168***

In The Beginning… **173**

The Golden Age **175**

Great Flood(s)... 177

The Reality Program 179

Religion 182

Simulation Pontification *183*

'The LCS Loves You' 184

Get in the Game...*186*

Afterward...*191*

Virtual Reality

If a tree falls in the forest and no one is around to hear it, does it make a sound?

The answer is no.

There is no tree, just as there is no forest. Our physical **reality is virtual**, and part of a much larger *reality system*.

Merriam-webster.com defines *"virtual reality"* as *"an **artificial environment** which is experienced through **sensory stimuli** (such as sights and sounds) **provided by a computer** and in which **one's actions** partially **determine what happens in the environment."***

Prior to the 1980s, our conception of *virtual reality* was essentially non-existent. First-person video games, such as *Space Invaders* and *Pong*, as basic as they now seem, allowed us to experience reality *virtually*. Since then, video games and other virtual-reality applications are quickly becoming indistinguishable from our physical reality.

'The Sims'

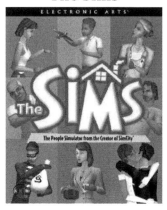

The Sims is a video game in which game-players live virtual lives within a virtual-reality simulation; interacting with others and using information to make choices.

The Sims characters inhabit a world of data, bound by rules, parameters, and limitations established within the game's computer code.

Data being transmitted between a server and the players creates a virtual world, rife with possibilities and potential.

Imagine being born into a multi-player virtual-reality simulation similar to *The Sims*.

Inside **this** virtual reality, all senses are engaged, and there is no way to stop the game or switch players.

If we fall and scrape our knee, we bleed and feel pain.

This virtual-reality simulation is complex and 'real', giving us *almost* no reason to question its authenticity.

2

Simulation Prognostication

Dictionary.com defines *"simulation"* as *"the representation of the behavior or characteristics of one system through the use of another system, **especially <u>a computer program designed for the purpose</u>**."*

The idea that we live in a virtual reality is still considered fringe, though the concept is slowly making its way into the mainstream.

In 2003, acclaimed author and Oxford professor Nick Bostrom published a paper titled *'Are You Living in a Computer Simulation?'*, highlighting the idea that we are unknowing participants in an *"ancestor-simulation"*:

A technologically mature "posthuman" civilization would have enormous computing power. Based on this empirical fact, the simulation argument shows that at least one of the following propositions is true: (1) The fraction of human-level civilizations that reach a posthuman stage is very close to zero; (2) The fraction of posthuman civilizations that are interested in running ancestor-simulations is very close to zero; (3) The fraction of all people with our kind of experiences that are living in a simulation is very close to one.

*If (1) is true, then we will almost certainly go extinct before reaching posthumanity. If (2) is true, then there must be a strong convergence among the courses of advanced civilizations so that virtually none contains any relatively wealthy individuals who desire to run ancestor-simulations and are free to do so. If (3) is true, then **we almost certainly live in a simulation**. In the dark forest of our current ignorance, it seems sensible to apportion one's credence roughly evenly between (1), (2), and (3).*

Unless we are now living in a simulation, our descendants will almost certainly never run an ancestor-simulation.

Brian Whitworth, on his website *brianwhitworth.com*, describes himself as *"a registered psychologist cross-trained in computing."*

Whitworth was a classically trained University professor, but curiosity caused him to veer from the mainstream.

In a research paper titled '*The Physical World as a Virtual Reality*', Whitworth describes his findings:

*This paper explores the idea that **the universe is a virtual reality created by information processing,** and relates this strange idea to t**he findings of modern physics about the physical world**. The virtual reality concept is familiar to us from online worlds, but our world as a virtual reality is usually a subject for science fiction rather than science. **Yet logically the world could be an information simulation running on a multi-dimensional space-time screen**. Indeed, if the essence of the universe is information, matter, charge, energy and movement could be aspects of information, and the many conservation laws could be a single law of information conservation.*

If the universe were a virtual reality, its creation at the big bang would no longer be paradoxical, as every virtual system must be booted up. It is suggested that whether the world is an objective reality or a virtual reality is a matter for science to resolve. **Modern information science can suggest how core physical properties like space, time, light, matter and movement could derive from information processing. Such an approach could reconcile relativity and quantum theories,** *with the former being* **<u>how information processing creates space-time, and the latter how it creates energy and matter.</u>**

MIT professor Seth Lloyd, in a 2016 *BBC.com* article titled '*We might live in a computer program, but it may not matter*', expresses a similar sentiment:

"The Universe can be regarded as a giant quantum computer," *says Seth Lloyd of the Massachusetts Institute of Technology. "If one looks at the 'guts' of the Universe – the structure of matter at its smallest scale – then* **<u>those guts consist of nothing more than [quantum] bits undergoing local, digital operations."</u>**

In his 2013 research paper titled '*The Universe as Quantum Computer*', Lloyd elaborates on his findings:

This article reviewed the history of computation with the goal of answering the question, 'Is the universe a computer?' The inability of classical digital computers to reproduce quantum effects efficiently makes it implausible that the universe is a classical digital system such as a cellular automaton. **However, all observed phenomena are consistent with the model in which the universe is a quantum computer, e.g., a quantum cellular automaton. The quantum computational model of the universe explains previously unexplained features,** *most importantly,* **<u>the co-existence in the universe of randomness and order, and of simplicity and complexity.</u>**

'Science'

Dictionary.com defines *"science"* as *"systematic knowledge of the physical or material world gained through **observation and experimentation.**"*

Scientific breakthroughs and innovations are responsible for drastically improving living conditions throughout the world. Scientific processes such as water filtration and sanitation helped curb the spread of disease, and science-based technological advances have enabled us to hold a computer in the palm of our hands.

Science is essential for understanding how things are, but offers few explanations as to 'why' they are that way.

Science can measure and describe certain properties of matter, but cannot explain how matter is created.

Science can measure the speed of light, but cannot explain the cause.

Science tells us that *dark matter* and *dark energy* make up the majority of our physical universe, but offers no logical explanation surrounding their cause, or *source*. A *nasa.gov* article titled '*Dark Energy, Dark Matter*' demonstrates how mainstream science offers no explanation for these *fundamental scientific principles:*

What Is Dark Energy?

*More is unknown than is known. We know how much dark energy there is because we know how it affects the universe's expansion. **<u>Other than that, it is a complete mystery</u>**. But it is an important mystery. **It turns out that roughly 68% of the universe is dark energy. Dark matter makes up about 27%.** The rest - everything on Earth, everything ever observed with all of our instruments, all normal matter - adds up to less than 5% of the universe. Come to think of it, maybe it shouldn't be called "normal" matter at all, since it is such a small fraction of the universe.*

Modern science claims to have the answers to **all** fundamental scientific matters, while stubbornly clinging to 'unscientific' *beliefs.*

The Scientific Revolution, influenced by Isaac Newton's *Laws of Motion*, brought the concept of an '*objective*' reality to the fore.

An '*objective*' reality posits that reality exists independent of the observer, and that all physics-related phenomena have a physical and absolute explanation and cause.

Newton's *Third Law of Motion* embodies the '*objective*' view of reality, proclaiming: "*For **every** action, there is an equal and opposite re-action.*"

French Scholar Pierre-Simon Laplace (1749-1827) helped solidify the '*objective*' view of reality. In '*A Philosophical Essay on Probabilities*', Laplace outlines the prevailing **belief** that *matter is life, and life is matter:*

We may regard the present state of the universe as the effect of its past and the cause of its future. *An intellect which at a certain moment would know all forces that set nature in motion, and all positions of all items of which nature is composed, if this intellect were also vast enough to submit these data to analysis, it would embrace in **a single formula the movements of the greatest bodies of the universe and those of the tiniest atom; for such an intellect <u>nothing would be uncertain</u> <u>and the future just like the past would be present before its eyes.</u>***

An '*objective*' view of reality *believes* in *material reductionism;* that physical matter is the fundamental nature of reality.

While the mainstream still clings to an '*objective*' model of reality, scientific *observation and experimentation* demonstrate that reality is instead '*subjective*', and **virtual** in nature.

Weird Science

*"The common sense view of the world in terms of objects that really exist "out there" independently of our observations **totally collapses in the face of the quantum factor**." –* Physicist Niels Bohr (1922 *Nobel Prize* Winner)

'Weird science' is a term given to scientific anomalies which defy the *accepted* laws of physics.

These scientific discoveries – which spawned the field of quantum mechanics - are considered mysterious and strange, and most 'scientists' simply ignore their astounding implications.

Quantum mechanics/physics plays a large role in our daily lives, demonstrating that *'weird science'* is much more practical than the name implies.

A 2015 article on *forbes.com* titled *'What Has Quantum Mechanics Ever Done For Us?'* demonstrates that *'weird science'* **is** responsible for society's rapid technological advancement:

*Desktops, laptops, tablets, smartphones, even small household appliances and kids' toys are driven by **computer chips that simply would not be possible to make without our modern understanding of quantum physics.***

*So, while it may sometimes seem like quantum physics is arcane and remote from everyday experience (a self-inflicted problem for physicists, to some degree, **as we often over-emphasize the weirder aspects when talking about quantum mechanics**), <u>**in fact it is absolutely essential to modern life**</u>. Semiconductor electronics, lasers, atomic clocks, and magnetic resonance scanners **all <u>fundamentally depend on our understanding of the quantum nature of light and matter</u>**.*

To further demonstrate the fundamental importance of quantum mechanics, *IBM* – one of the largest technology companies in the world – understands that quantum computing is the future, and not a '*weird*' scientific anomaly.

On their website, *ibm.com*, the topic of quantum computing is outlined:

'What is Quantum Computing?'

*Quantum computers are **incredibly powerful machines** that take a **new approach** to processing information. Built on the principles of quantum mechanics, they exploit **complex and fascinating laws of nature that are <u>always there, but usually remain hidden from view</u>**. By harnessing such natural behavior, quantum computing can run new types of algorithms to **process information more holistically**. They may one day lead to **revolutionary breakthroughs** in materials and drug discovery, the optimization of complex manmade systems, and artificial intelligence. We expect them to open doors that we once **thought would remain locked indefinitely**. Acquaint yourself with the **strange and exciting** world of quantum computing.*

While the mainstream is beginning to understand the importance and implications of quantum mechanics, these "*strange and exciting*" concepts have been documented since the 1920s.

Heisenberg

"*Not only is the Universe stranger than we think, **it is stranger than we can think**.*" — Werner Heisenberg; '*Across the Frontiers*'

At the core of our physical reality, there is *uncertainty*.

German scientist Werner Heisenberg won the 1932 *Nobel Prize* in physics. Credited with coining the Heisenberg '*uncertainty principle*', Heisenberg found that **physical particles aren't really 'real'**:

"**The atoms or elementary particles themselves <u>are not real</u>; they form a world of potentialities or possibilities rather than one of things or facts.**"

The *uncertainty principle* demonstrates that we can measure where a particle is, or where it is going, **but never both simultaneously**.

A 2013 article on *theguardian.com* titled '*What is Heisenberg's*

11

Uncertainty Principle?' **attempts** to explain the phenomenon, while also acknowledging that the results are not consistent with how a fundamentally physical reality should behave:

*One way to think about the uncertainty principle is as an extension of how we see and measure things in the everyday world. You can read these words because particles of light, photons, have bounced off the screen or paper and reached your eyes. Each photon on that path carries with it some **information** about the surface it has bounced from, at the speed of light. Seeing a subatomic particle, such as an electron, is not so simple. You might similarly bounce a photon off it and then hope to detect that photon with an instrument. But chances are that the photon will impart some momentum to the electron as it hits it and change the path of the particle you are trying to measure. Or else, given that quantum particles often move so fast, the electron may no longer be in the place it was when the photon originally bounced off it. Either way, **your observation of either position or momentum will be inaccurate and, more important, <u>the act of observation affects the particle being observed.</u>***

<u>The uncertainty principle is at the heart of many things that we observe but cannot explain using classical (non-quantum) physics.</u>

Tunneling

"**Everything we call real is made of things that cannot be regarded as
real**. If quantum mechanics hasn't profoundly shocked you, you haven't
understood it yet." – Physicist Niels Bohr (*Nobel Prize* Winner; 1922)

The concept of *tunneling* is another quantum mechanics *mystery*,
demonstrating that our physical reality is not fundamentally physical.

Tunneling demonstrates that particles – which mainstream science
deems to be pieces of physical matter – are able to penetrate
"*impassible*" barriers.

AZoQuantum.com ascribes to be "*the leading online publication for the
Quantum Science community.*"

An article on *Azoquantum.com* titled *'An Introduction to Quantum
Tunneling'* outlines this *'strange'* phenomenon:

*The quantum tunneling effect is, as the name suggests, a quantum
phenomenon which occurs when **particles move through a barrier that
should be impossible to move through** according to classical physics.*

The barrier can be a <u>physically impassable medium</u>, *like an insulator or a vacuum, or it can be a region of high potential energy.*

In classical mechanics, if a particle has insufficient energy to overcome a potential barrier, it simply won't. In the quantum world, however, **<u>particles can often behave like waves</u>.**

This "*impossible*" feat is so predictable and probabilistic that *quantum tunneling* has numerous real-world applications, including deleting data from flash drives.

'The Wave'

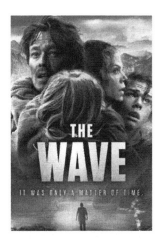

The idea that *'particles behave like waves'* is used to explain why light *performs* as a non-physical wave and as a tiny piece of physical matter - *at the same time* - according to Newtonian physics.

An article on *physics.info* titled *'The Nature of Waves'* describes the *bizarre* properties of waves:

*Waves transfer energy, momentum, and **information, but not mass**.*

The paradoxical behavior of particles sometimes acting like particles and sometimes acting like waves is referred to as *'wave-particle duality'*. Albert Einstein outlines the *"two contradictory pictures of reality"*:

*It seems as though we must use sometimes the one theory and sometimes the other, while at times we may use either. **We are faced with a new kind of difficulty. We have two contradictory pictures of reality; separately neither of them fully explains the phenomena of light, but together they do.***

An article on *physicsclassroom.com* titled *'What is a Wave?'* further elaborates on the *bizarre* nature of waves:

*A wave can be described as **<u>a disturbance that travels through a medium, transporting energy from one location (its source) to another location without transporting matter. Each individual particle of the medium is temporarily displaced</u>** and then returns to its original equilibrium positioned.*

Mainstream science accepts that *waves* are a fundamental aspect of our physical reality, while quietly ignoring the fact that particles, or 'physical matter', cannot be *magically transported* through *"impassable barriers"* in an *'objective'* physical reality.

Quantum Entanglement

In the 1930s, *'quantum entanglement'* blew another hole in the *'objective'* model of reality.

Quantum entanglement demonstrates that disparate 'physical' particles, separated by *unlimited distances*, **act as one**.

A 2015 article on *nature.com* titled *'Quantum 'spookiness' passes toughest test yet'* describes how this 'physically impossible' phenomenon is still considered a mystery to mainstream science:

*It's a bad day both for Albert Einstein and for hackers. The most rigorous test of quantum theory ever carried out has confirmed that the **'spooky action at a distance'** that the German physicist famously hated — in which **manipulating one object instantaneously seems to affect another, far away one — is an inherent part of the quantum world.***

*The experiment, performed in the Netherlands, could be the **final nail in the coffin for models of the atomic world** that are more intuitive than standard quantum mechanics, say some physicists.*

The *'spooky action at a distance'*, as Einstein referred to it, defies the speed of light, demonstrating that this fundamental *natural* process cannot be explained by 'classical physics' (the article continues):

In quantum mechanics, **objects can be in multiple states simultaneously***: for example, an atom can be in two places, or spin in opposite directions, at once. Measuring an object forces it to snap into a well-defined state.* *Furthermore, th****e properties of*** <u>***different objects***</u> <u>***can become 'entangled', meaning that their states are linked***</u>*: when a property of one such object is measured, the properties of all its entangled twins become set, too.*

This idea galled Einstein because it seemed that **this ghostly influence** *would be transmitted* **instantaneously** *between even vastly separated but entangled particles — implying that it could* <u>**contravene the universal rule that nothing can travel faster than the speed of light**</u>*. He proposed that quantum particles do have set properties before they are measured, called* **hidden variables***. And even though those variables cannot be accessed, he suggested that* **they** <u>**pre-program**</u> **entangled particles to behave in correlated ways.**

To Kill a Cat

"**We do not belong to this material world that science constructs for us**. *We are not in it;* **we are outside**. *We are only spectators. The reason why we believe that we are in it, that we belong to the picture, is that our bodies are in the picture. Our bodies belong to it. Not only my own body, but those of my friends, also of my dog and cat and horse, and of all the other people and animals*. And this is my only means of communicating with them." — Erwin Schrödinger; 'Nature and the Greeks' and 'Science and Humanism'

Erwin Schrödinger (1887-1961), winner of the 1933 *Nobel Prize* in physics, is best known for the *Schrödinger's cat* analogy.

A 2002 article on *discover.com* titled '*Does the Universe Exist if We're Not Looking?*' describes the *strange* paradox:

Put a cat in a closed box, along with a vial of poison gas, a piece of uranium, and a Geiger counter hooked up to a hammer suspended above the gas vial. During the course of the experiment, the radioactive uranium may or may not emit a particle. If the particle is released, the Geiger counter will detect it and send a signal to a mechanism controlling the hammer, which will strike the vial and release the gas, killing the cat. If the particle is not released, the cat will live. Schrödinger asked, What could be known about the cat before opening the box?

*If there were no such thing as quantum mechanics, the answer would be simple: The cat is either alive or dead, depending on whether a particle hit the Geiger counter. But in the quantum world, things are not so straightforward. **The particle and the cat now form a quantum system consisting of all possible outcomes of the experiment.** One outcome includes a dead cat; another, a live one. **Neither becomes real until someone opens the box and looks inside.** With that **observation**, an entire consistent sequence of events— the particle jettisoned from the uranium, the release of the poison gas, the cat's death— **at once becomes real, giving the appearance of something that has taken weeks to transpire.** Stanford University physicist Andrei Linde believes this quantum paradox gets to the heart of Wheeler's idea about the nature of the universe: **The principles of quantum mechanics dictate severe limits on the certainty of our knowledge.***

*"You may ask whether the universe really existed before you start looking at it," he says. "That's the same Schrödinger cat question. And my answer would be that **the universe looks as if it existed before I started looking at it.** When you open the cat's box after a week, you're going to find either a live cat or a smelly piece of meat. You can say that the cat looks as if it were dead or as if it were alive during the whole week. Likewise, when we look at the universe, the best we can say is that it looks as if it were there 10 billion years ago."*

The Double-Slit Experiment

"*We choose to examine a phenomenon which is **impossible, absolutely impossible, to explain in any classical way, and which has in it the heart of quantum mechanics. In reality, it contains the only mystery.** We cannot make the mystery go away by "explaining" how it works. We will just tell you how it works. In telling you how it works we will have told you about the basic peculiarities of all quantum mechanics.*" - Physicist Richard Feynman (1965 *Nobel Prize* in physics; referring to the *double-slit experiment*)

The *double-slit experiment* clearly demonstrates that **reality is virtual**. The *double-slit experiment* demonstrates that our environment, or our *physical reality*, behaves differently **when we aren't interacting with it**.

This strange enigma cannot be explained by classical physics, bringing the *quantum* factor to the fore.

The following illustration (courtesy of Wikipedia) of the *double-slit experiment* demonstrates how an "*electron*", defined by *Dictionary.com* as "*an elementary particle that is a **fundamental constituent of matter,**"* behaves differently when it is being measured, or observed, than when it is not.

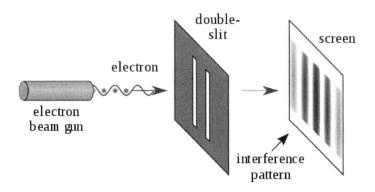

In the experiment, *a random particle generator* fires off electrons towards a back screen (reference the "screen" in the illustration), with another wall containing two slits (reference the "double-slit" wall in the illustration) in-between the particle generator (reference the "electron beam gun" in the illustration) and the back screen.

When **no** measuring device is set-up to determine which slit each electron travels though prior to hitting the back wall, the electrons act as 'waves', hitting the back screen in a *diffraction, or "interference pattern"* (shown in the illustration) – and not travelling directly through one of the two slits, as a piece of physical matter *should*.

Dictionary.com defines *"diffraction pattern"* as *"**the bending of waves**, especially sound and light waves, **around obstacles in their path**."*

Mysteriously, when the experiment is modified to observe, or measure, exactly which slit each electron travels through prior hitting the back screen, the electrons only hit the back screen directly behind one of the two slits, *performing* exactly like a piece of physical matter should.

A 2002 article on *discovermagazine.com* titled *'Does the Universe Exist if We're Not Looking?'* describes the *double-slit experiment*:

*It illustrates a key principle of quantum mechanics: **Light has a dual nature.** Sometimes light behaves like a compact particle, a photon;*

*sometimes it seems to behave like a wave spread out in space, **just like the ripples in a pond**. In the experiment, light — a stream of photons — shines through two parallel slits and hits a strip of photographic film behind the slits. The experiment can be run two ways: with photon detectors right beside each slit that allow physicists to observe the photons as they pass, or with detectors removed, which allows the photons to travel unobserved. **When physicists use the photon detectors, the result is unsurprising: Every photon is observed to pass through one slit or the other. The photons, in other words, act like particles.***

The article continues, explaining that taking a *measurement of the data* changes the way photons behave:

*But when the photon detectors are removed, **something weird occurs**. One would expect to see two distinct clusters of dots on the film, corresponding to where individual photons hit after randomly passing through one slit or the other. Instead, **a pattern of alternating light and dark stripes appears**. Such a pattern could be produced only if the photons are behaving like waves, with each individual photon spreading out and surging against both slits at once, like a breaker hitting a jetty. Alternating bright stripes in the pattern on the film show where crests from those waves overlap; dark stripes indicate that a crest and a trough have canceled each other.*

The outcome of the experiment depends on what the physicists try to measure: If they set up detectors beside the slits, the photons act like ordinary particles, always traversing one route or the other, not both at the same time. In that case the striped pattern doesn't appear on the film. But if the physicists remove the detectors, each photon seems to travel both routes simultaneously like a tiny wave, producing the striped pattern.

Mainstream science still attempts to paint the experiment with a *physical-matter* brush, claiming that the particles go through both slits "*simultaneously*," though no physical evidence supports that claim.

University of Oxford University professor Marcus du Sautoy has been studying mathematics and quantum mechanics for many years, holding numerous awards and distinctions. In his 2017 book *'The Great Unknown: Seven Journeys to the Frontiers of Science'*, he outlines the effect of *the observer*:

The wave quality of light is the same as that of the electron. The wave determines the probable location of the photon of light when it is detected. The wave character of light is not vibrating stuff like a wave of water but rather a wavelike function **_encoding information about where you'll find the photon of light once it is detected_**. *Until it reaches the detector plate, like the electron, it is* **seemingly passing through both slits simultaneously**, *making its mind up about its location only once it is observed [...].*
It's this act of observation that is such a strange feature of quantum physics. *Until I ask the detector to pick up where the electron is, the particle should be thought of as probabilistically distributed over space, with a probability described by a mathematical function that has wavelike characteristics. The effect of the two slits on this mathematical wave function alters it in such a way that the electron is forbidden from being located at some points on the detector plate.* **_But when the particle is observed, the die is cast, probabilities disappear, and the particle must decide on a location_**.

Nobel Prize winning physicist Richard Feynman (1918-1988) outlines some of the fundamental questions surrounding *the observer effect*, such as who or what qualifies as an 'observer', while highlighting the *weird* implications:

This is all very confusing, especially when we consider that **even though we may consistently consider ourselves to be the outside observer when we look at the rest of the world, the rest of the world is at the same time observing us, and** *that* **often we agree on what we see in each other**. *Does this then mean that my observations become real only when I observe an observer observing something as it happens? This is a horrible viewpoint.* **Do you seriously entertain the idea that _without the_**

24

**observer there is no reality?** _Which observer? Any observer? Is a fly an observer? Is a star an observer? Was there no reality in the universe before 10^9 B.C. when life began? Or_ **_are you the observer? Then there is no reality to the world after you are dead? I know a number of otherwise respectable physicists who have bought life insurance._**

Delayed Choice

*"**No phenomenon is a real phenomenon until it is an observed phenomenon**."* – Physicist John Archibald Wheeler (1911-2008)

The *delayed choice quantum eraser experiment*, which takes the *double-slit experiment* a step further, demonstrates that **reality does not exist until it is measured, or recorded, by a conscious *observer*,** regardless of how much time has elapsed from the original event.

A 2015 article on *phys.org* titled *'Experiment confirms quantum theory weirdness'* describes this *reality-bending* conclusion, which is only possible in **a virtual-reality simulation:**

The bizarre nature of reality as laid out by quantum theory has survived another test, with scientists performing a famous experiment and proving that <u>reality does not exist until it is measured</u>.

*Physicists at The Australian National University (ANU) have conducted **John Wheeler's delayed-choice thought experiment**, which involves a moving object that is **given the choice to act like a particle or a wave**. Wheeler's experiment then asks - at which point does the object decide?*

Common sense says the object is either wave-like or particle-like, independent of how we measure it. <u>But quantum physics predicts that whether you observe wave like behavior (interference) or particle behavior (no interference) depends only on how it is actually measured at the end of its journey</u>. This is exactly what the ANU team found.

"<u>It proves that measurement is everything. At the quantum level, reality does not exist if you are not looking at it</u>," said Associate Professor Andrew Truscott from the ANU Research School of Physics and Engineering.

26

Associate Professor Truscott describes the implications of these experimentally-confirmed results (the article continues):

"**<u>The atoms did not travel from A to B</u>. It was only when <u>they were measured</u>** at the end of the journey that their wave-like or particle-like behavior was **<u>brought into existence</u>,**" he said.

A *popularmechanics.com* article titled '*The Logic-Defying Double-Slit Experiment Is Even Weirder Than You Thought*' confirms these *bizarre* findings:

A group of scientists tried a variation on the double slit experiment, called the **delayed choice experiment.** The scientists placed a special crystal at each slit. The crystal splits any incoming photons into a pair of identical photons. One photon from this pair should go on to create the standard interference pattern, while the other travels to a detector. Perhaps with this setup, physicists might successfully find a way to observe **the logic-defying behavior of photons**.

But it still doesn't work. And here's the really weird part: I**t doesn't work regardless of when that detection happens. Even if the second photon is detected after the first photon hits the screen, it still ruins the interference pattern. This means that observing a photon can change events that have already happened.**

Scientists are still unsure how exactly this whole thing works. It's one of the greatest mysteries of quantum mechanics. Perhaps <u>someday</u> someone will finally be able to solve it.

Mainstream science has all but given up on understanding these fundamental attributes of our reality.

A 2016 *popularmechanics.com* article titled '*The Double-Slit Experiment That Blew Open Quantum Mechanics*' demonstrates how mainstream science is insistent on assigning a 'physical' explanation to non-physical phenomena:

*We can't fully explain these phenomena **yet,** but we can observe them. It is only a matter of time before someone comes up with the correct mathematical equations to fully predict and model these events, and **when they do**, the third major <u>**set of physical laws**</u> will be born.*

Let's Get Digital

"Digital mechanics predicts that for every continuous symmetry of physics there will be some microscopic process that violates that symmetry." – Physicist Edward Fredkin

Digital physics , or *digital mechanics*, posits that reality is based off of **information**, and not tiny physical pieces of matter.

Distinguished *Carnegie Mellon University* professor Edward Fredkin is a pioneer and proponent of *digital physics*, as well as its contemplative counterpart, *digital philosophy*.

A 1988 article on t*heatlantic.com* titled '*Did the Universe Just Happen'* describes how information/data is at the core of everything we consider to be 'physical':

*Fredkin works in a twilight zone of modern science—the interface of computer science and physics. Here two concepts that traditionally have ranked among science's most fundamental—matter and energy—keep bumping into a third: **information**. The exact relationship among the three is a question without a clear answer, a question vague enough, and basic enough, to have inspired a wide variety of opinions. Some* *scientists have settled for modest and sober answers. Information, they will tell you, is just one of many forms of matter and energy; it is embodied in things like a computer's electrons and a brain's neural firings, things like newsprint and radio waves, and that is that. Others talk in grander terms, suggesting that information deserves full equality with matter and energy, that it should join them in some sort of scientific trinity, that these three things are the main ingredients of reality.*

*Fredkin goes further still. According to his theory of digital physics, **<u>information is more fundamental than matter and energy</u>**. He believes that atoms, electrons, and quarks **<u>consist ultimately of bits</u>—binary units of information, like those that are the currency of computation in a personal computer or a pocket calculator.** And he believes that the behavior of those bits, and thus of **the entire universe, is governed by a single programming rule.** This rule, Fredkin says, is something fairly simple, something **vastly less arcane than the mathematical constructs that conventional physicists use to explain the dynamics of physical reality.** Yet through **ceaseless repetition—<u>by tirelessly taking information it has just transformed and transforming it further</u>—it has <u>generated pervasive complexity</u>**. Fredkin calls this rule, with discernible reverence, "**the cause and prime mover of everything**."*

'It from Bit'

*"**The universe does not exist "out there,"** independent of us. **We are inescapably involved in bringing about that which appears to be happening. We are not only observers. We are participators. In some strange sense, <u>this is a participatory universe</u>**. Physics is no longer satisfied with insights only into particles, fields of force, into geometry, or even into time and space. **Today we demand of physics some understanding of existence itself**."* –Physicist John Archibald Wheeler

John Archibald Wheeler (1911-2008) was a professor of physics at *Princeton University* from 1938 through 1976, and an influential and respected member of the physics community throughout his life.

Wheeler coined the phrase *'it from bit'*, outlining the concept in a 1990 research paper titled *'Information, Physics, Quantum: The Search for Links'*:

It from bit** symbolizes the idea that every item of the physical world has at bottom — at a very deep bottom, in most instances — **<u>an immaterial source and explanation</u>; that which we call reality arises in the last analysis from the posing of yes-no questions** and the registering of equipment-evoked responses; in short, that **<u>all things physical are information-theoretic in origin and that this is a participatory universe.</u>

Credited with designing the *delayed choice experiment*, Wheeler describes how our 'physical' reality is not truly physical:

*The thing that causes people to argue about when and how the photon learns that the experimental apparatus is in a certain configuration and then changes from wave to particle to fit the demands of the experiment's configuration is **<u>the assumption that a photon had some physical form before the astronomers observed it.</u>** Either it was a wave*

31

*or a particle; either it went both ways around the galaxy or only one way. Actually, **<u>quantum phenomena are neither waves nor particles but are intrinsically undefined until the moment they are measured.</u>***

'The One'

*"When we speak of man, we have a conception of **humanity as a whole**, and before applying scientific methods to the investigation of his movement we must accept this as **a <u>physical fact</u>**. But can anyone doubt to-day that all the millions of individuals and all the innumerable types and characters constitute an entity, a unit? **Though free to think and act, <u>we are held together</u>**, like the stars in the firmament, with ties inseparable. These ties cannot be seen, but we can feel them. I cut myself in the finger, and it pains me: this finger is a part of me. I see a friend hurt, and it hurts me, too: my friend and I are one...**Does this not prove that each of us is only part of a whole**?"* – Nikola Tesla (1900)

The idea that everything is connected is not a new concept, nor is it confined to eastern religions or 'new-age' philosophies.

Russian author Fyodor Dostoevsky (1821-1881), who Albert Einstein describes as a *"great religious writer,"* understood that everything is inter-related. In his 1879 book *'The Brothers Karamazov'*, Dostoevsky describes our inherent connection:

My brother asked the birds to forgive him: that sounds senseless, but it is right; for all is like an ocean, all is flowing and blending; a touch in one place sets up movement at the other end of the earth. It may be senseless to beg forgiveness of the birds, but birds would be happier at your side –a little happier, anyway– and children and all animals, if you yourself were nobler than you are now. It's all like an ocean, I tell you. Then you would pray to the birds too, consumed by an all-embracing love in a sort of transport, and pray that they too will forgive you your sin.

Walter Russell was described by the *New York Herald Tribune* in 1963 as "*the modern Leonardo*," due to his wide-ranging contributions to art, science and philosophy.

Russell's 1926 book titled '*The Universal One*' attempts to bridge the disparate fields of science and religion.

In the prelude, Russell describes the attributes of '*the one*':

This is a universe of Mind, a finite universe, *limited as to cause, and to the effect of cause. A finite universe, in which the effects of cause are limited, must also be limited as to cause; so when that measurable cause is known, then can man comprehend and measure all effects. The effects of cause are complex and mystify man, but cause itself is simple. The universe is a multiplicity of changing effects of **but One unchanging cause. All things are universal. Nothing is which is not universal. Nothing is of itself alone. Man and Mind and all creating things are universal. No man can say: 'I alone am I.' <u>There is but One universe, One Mind, One force, One substance</u>. When man knows this in measurable exactness then will he have no limitations within those which are universal**.*

The idea that *everything* is connected is at direct odds with the notion of an '*objective*' physical reality.

'The End of Science'

"As far as **the laws** of mathematics refer to reality, they are not certain; and as far as they are certain, **they do not refer to reality**." — Albert Einstein

Quantum mechanics has quietly disproven Albert Einstein's *Theory of Relativity*, demonstrating that reality is not *relative* at the quantum level.

In his 2017 book titled *'The Great Unknown: Seven Journeys to the Frontiers of Science'*, Oxford professor Marcus du Sautoy describes the mainstream's dismay with the underlying *quantum mysteries*:

*To understand this new frontier, I will have to try to master one of the most difficult and counterintuitive theories ever recorded in the annals of science: quantum physics. Listen to those who have spent their lives immersed in this world and you will have a sense of the challenge we face. After making his groundbreaking discoveries in quantum physics, Werner Heisenberg recalled, "I repeated to myself again and again the question: **Can nature possibly be so absurd as it seemed to us in these*** *atomic experiments?" Einstein declared after one discovery, "**If it is correct it signifies the end of science.**" Schrödinger was so shocked by the implications of what he'd cooked up that he admitted, "I do not like it and I am sorry I had anything to do with it." Nevertheless, quantum physics is now one of the most __**powerful and well-tested pieces of science on the books.**__ **Nothing has come close to pushing it off its pedestal as one of the great scientific achievements of the last century.** So there is nothing to do but to dive headfirst into this uncertain world. Feynman has some good advice for me as I embark on my quest: "**I am going to tell you what nature behaves like. If you will simply admit that maybe she does behave like this, you will find her a delightful, entrancing thing. Do not keep saying to yourself, if you can possibly avoid it, 'But how can it be like that?' because you will get 'down the drain,' into a blind alley from which nobody has yet escaped. Nobody knows how it can be like that**.*

Mainstream science's insistence on physical explanations has caused some strange and illogical conclusions to be drawn.

The *"multiverse"* concept posits that there are infinite physical realities, with separate physical realities continuously created for *every* minute variable change.

A 2012 article on *space.com* titled '*5 Reasons We May Live in a Multiverse*' highlights the persistence of mainstream science to prove that we are *living in a material world*:

*But if space-time goes on forever, **then it must start repeating at some point, because there are a finite number of ways __particles__ can be arranged in space and time.***

*So if you look far enough, you would encounter another version of you — in fact, __**infinite versions of you**__. Some of these twins will be doing exactly what you're doing right now, while others will have worn a different sweater this morning, and still others will have made vastly* *different career and life choices.*

Someone born into a virtual-reality video game would not be able to determine who created the game, or how it was created, using the *physical-reality* resources within the game.

To understand quantum mechanics and the true nature of our reality, **we are forced to look beyond the physical.**

Quantum physics does not signify '*the end of science*', but instead provides a more accurate and scientific approach to understanding the fundamental nature of reality.

Modern science has all but given up on the elusive big '*theory of everything*', **while others present a working model.**

'My Big Toe'

*"From all we have learnt about the structure of living matter, we must be prepared to find it working in a manner that cannot be reduced to the ordinary laws of physics. And that not on the ground that there is any "new force" or what not, directing the behavior of the single atoms within a living organism, but **because the construction is different from anything we have yet tested in the physical laboratory.**"* - Erwin Schrödinger (1887-1961), winner of the 1933 *Nobel Prize* in physics

Physicist **Thomas Campbell** incorporates science, logic, and first-hand experience to demonstrate that our physical reality is indeed a virtual reality.

Campbell partnered with Bob Monroe, author of three consciousness-related books, as well as the founder of the *Monroe Institute*, whose stated mission is to advance *"the exploration of human consciousness and the experience of expanded states of awareness as a path to creating a life of personal freedom, meaning, insight, and happiness."*

The *Monroe Institute*'s website, *monroeinstitute.org*, outlines Tom Campbell's background and contributions to the organization:

*Tom Campbell, a nuclear physicist, began researching altered states of consciousness with Bob Monroe Journeys out Of the Body, Far Journeys, and The Ultimate Journey at Monroe Laboratories in the early 1970s **where he and a few others were instrumental in getting Monroe's laboratory for the study of consciousness up and running. These early drug-free consciousness pioneers helped design experiments, developed the technology for creating specific altered states, and were the main subjects of study (guinea pigs) all at the same time. Tom is the "TC (physicist)" described in Bob Monroe's second book Far Journeys.***

Campbell has been a serious explorer of the frontiers of reality, mind, consciousness, and psychic phenomena for the last forty years. Using his acquired mastery of the <u>Out Of Body Experience as a research tool</u>, Campbell focused his work toward discovering the outer boundaries, inner workings, and causal dynamics of the larger reality system. <u>The result of this research unites the worlds of objective and subjective experience under one scientific explanation, thus, achieving the goal of generating one unified, comprehensive theory of everything (TOE) that bridges metaphysics and physics with one scientific understanding.</u>

*In February of 2003, Tom published the My Big TOE trilogy (MBT) which represents the results and conclusions of his scientific exploration of the nature of existence. This overarching model of reality, mind, and consciousness explains the paranormal as well as the normal, **places spirituality within a scientific context**, solves a host of scientific paradoxes and provides direction for those wishing to personally experience an expanded awareness of All That Is. **The MBT reality model explains metaphysics, spirituality, love, and human purpose at the most fundamental level, provides a <u>complete theory of consciousness</u>, and <u>solves the outstanding fundamental physics problems of our time</u>**, deriving both relativity theory and quantum mechanics from first principles – something traditional physics cannot yet do. <u>As a logic-based work of science, My Big TOE has no basis in belief, dogma, or any unusual assumptions.</u>*

Tom Campbell's *Big Theory of Everything,* laid out in his three-book set titled '*My Big Toe*' (available for free on Google books), demonstrates that the commonly-used equation for realty, $E = mc^2$, is not a legitimate real-world scientific explanation for *everything*.

A *bbc.co.uk* article titled '*What the general theory of relativity doesn't explain*' describes how the theory of relativity, which is generally accepted as **the** '*theory of everything*', "*falls apart*" in the face of quantum mechanics:

General relativity works well on the scale it is usually applied, for example planets, **but falls apart for very small and very large applications.**

The equations of general relativity don't work on very small scales. Here**, quantum mechanics reigns, and searching for a quantum theory of gravity which supersedes general relativity is a holy grail of modern science.**

Tom Campbell's *Big Theory of Everything* demonstrates that **R=I,** or **Reality** equals **Information**.

Campbell presents a working model, stressing the fact that this is simply a model, and **not intended to be, or become, a dogmatic approach to reality**.

'The Larger Consciousness System'

"Consciousness cannot be accounted for in physical terms. <u>For consciousness is absolutely fundamental</u>. It cannot be accounted for in terms of anything else." — Physicist Erwin Schrödinger (1887-1961; 1933 *Nobel Prize* in physics)

Tom Campbell's *Big Theory of Everything* describes the fundamental source of reality as '*the larger consciousness system*', or the '*LCS*'.

"Consciousness is the computer." – Tom Campbell

On his website, my-big-toe.com, Campbell defines '*the larger consciousness system*':

*The LCS is an **aware, imperfect, finite, evolving conscious entity in the form of a large digital information system. At the root, there is nothing but information – everything, every idea, thought, desire, feeling, emotion, star, rock, brain, atom, space and time can be reduced to information and all interaction reduced to communication**. Positing anything more is logically unnecessary (unnecessary assumptions and unnecessary complexity) since all can be directly derived from this single starting point. An understanding that, <u>**at the most fundamental level of our "physical" reality, there is nothing but information**</u> is an idea that science is now embracing more and more every day.*

The idea that consciousness is fundamental to our reality is not a new concept.

41

German physicist Max Planck (1858-1947) is credited with being the originator of 'quantum theory', which spawned quantum mechanics. Awarded the *Nobel Prize* in physics in 1918, Planck describes consciousness and how it pertains to the nature of reality:

*I regard **consciousness as fundamental**. **I regard matter as derivative from consciousness**. **We cannot get behind consciousness**. Everything that we talk about, everything that we regard as existing, postulates consciousness.*

Planck further elaborates on this *bizarre* idea:

There is no matter as such. *All matter originates and exists only by virtue of a force which **brings the particle of an atom to vibration and holds this most minute solar system of the atom together**. **We must assume behind this force the existence of a conscious and intelligent mind. This mind is the matrix of all matter.***

Planck, *'the founder of quantum theory'*, determined that **physical matter is derived from consciousness.**

Hungarian-American physicist Eugene Wigner, recipient of (half of) the 1963 *Nobel Prize* in physics, was also acutely interested in the study of consciousness.

Wigner described how mainstream science clings to *beliefs* which are disproven by experimental *quantum* evidence:

*The **doctrine that the world** is made up of objects whose existence is independent of human consciousness turns out to be in conflict with **quantum mechanics and with facts established by experiment.***

Wigner explains how consciousness is a logical and necessary component of quantum physics:

When the province of physical theory was extended to encompass microscopic phenomena through the creation of quantum mechanics, the concept of consciousness came to the fore again. ***It was not possible to formulate the laws of quantum mechanics in a fully consistent way without reference to the consciousness.***

In a paper titled *'Remarks on the Mind-Body Question'*, Wigner also concludes that *consciousness is fundamental:*

*It will remain remarkable, in whatever way our future concepts may develop, that the very study of the external world led to the conclusion that **the content of the consciousness is an ultimate reality**.*

The pioneers of quantum physics understood that our physical reality is a derivative of consciousness. Over time, that information has been ignored and forgotten.

Consciousness – 'The Hard Problem'

*"The centermost processes of the brain with which consciousness is presumably associated are simply not understood. **They are so far beyond our comprehension that no one I know of has been able to imagine their nature**."* – Roger Wolcott Sperry (1981 *Nobel Prize* recipient)

Mainstream science clings to the notion that consciousness is a byproduct of the brain, while there is no evidence to support the claim. In an *'objective'* deterministic reality, no options exist beyond the physical.

With no *'objective'* explanation, consciousness has been dubbed the *'hard problem'*, and largely ignored by mainstream science.

Newscientist.com, in a series titled *'Consciousness: The what, why and how'*, outlines the *"hard problem"* of consciousness:

*THERE are a lot of hard problems in the world, but only one of them gets to call itself "the hard problem". **And that is the problem of consciousness – <u>how a kilogram or so of nerve cells</u> conjures up the seamless kaleidoscope of sensations, thoughts, memories and emotions that occupy every waking moment.***

***The intractability of this problem** prompted British psychologist Stuart Sutherland's notorious 1989 observation: "Consciousness is a fascinating but elusive phenomenon… Nothing worth reading has been written on it."*

<u>The hard problem remains unsolved.</u>

Princeton University, the Ivy League college located in New Jersey (USA), studied consciousness for **nearly thirty years**.

The *Princeton Engineering Anomalies Research* (**PEAR**) program – which is archived at *https://web.archive.org/web/20171122092834/http://www.princeton.edu/~pear/* - described itself as the *"Scientific Study of Consciousness-Related Physical Phenomena."*

The *PEAR* program outlined their protocols, while boldly asserting that **physical reality is created by consciousness**:

*Studying the interaction of human consciousness with sensitive physical devices, systems, and processes, and developing complementary theoretical models to enable better **understanding of the role of consciousness in the establishment of physical reality.***

The conclusions drawn by the *PEAR* program – described on the *"Implications"* page - demonstrate that the mainstream conception of reality is **scientifically** flawed:

*PEAR's contribution to this expansion of the scientific worldview has been its **accumulation of huge bodies of consciousness-correlated empirical evidence that the subjective/objective dichotomy of Cartesian philosophy is no longer entirely viable.***

*More comprehensive accommodation of these anomalies within a functional scientific framework will require the **explicit inclusion of consciousness as an active agent in the establishment of physical reality**, a generalization of the scientific paradigm demanding more courageous theoretical structures **than are employed at present**, guided by more extensive empirical data than are now available, acquired via more **cooperative interdisciplinary collaborations** than are currently practiced. It is our hope that by its proposition of a few possible conceptual models PEAR has established productive precedents for such representation of this formidable, but crucial, topical domain.*

The Spiritual: Cultural Implications

45

Beyond its revolutionary technological applications and scientific impact, __*the evidence of an active role of consciousness in the establishment of physical reality*__ ***holds profound implications for our view of ourselves, our relationships to others, and to the cosmos in which we exist.*** *These, in turn, must inevitably impact our values, our priorities, our sense of responsibility, and our style of life. Our ability to acquire, or to generate* ***tangible, measurable information independent of distance or time challenges the foundation of any reductionist brain-based model of consciousness that may be invoked.*** *The lack of notable correlations in the data with standard learning curves or other recognizable cognitive patterns, combined with the repeatable and distinct gender-related differences, suggest that these* ***abilities may stem from a*** __***more fundamental source than heretofore suspected***__*.*

Certainly, there is little doubt that integration of these changes in ***our understanding of ourselves*** __***can lead to a substantially superior human ethic, wherein the long-estranged siblings of science and spirit, of analysis and aesthetics, of intellect and intuition, and of many other subjective and objective aspects of human experience can be productively reunited.***__

PEAR determined that **consciousness is fundamental** by following the scientific protocols that would be expected from an elite educational institution.

PEAR summarized some of their key findings (outlined on the "*Experiments*" page of their archived site):

The most substantial portion of the PEAR experimental program examined anomalies arising in human/machine interactions.

In these studies human operators attempted to bias the output of a variety of mechanical, electronic, optical, acoustical, and fluid devices to ***conform to pre-stated intentions, without recourse to any known physical influences.*** *In unattended calibrations all of these sophisticated machines produced strictly random data, yet the experimental results display increases in* __***information content that can only be attributed to the consciousness of their human operators.***__

Over the laboratory's 28-year history, <u>thousands of such experiments,</u>
<u>involving many millions of trials, were performed by several hundred</u>
<u>operators</u>. The observed effects were usually quite small, of the order of
*a few parts in ten thousand on average, <u>**but they compounded to highly**</u>*
*<u>**significant statistical deviations from chance expectations**</u>. These*
results are summarized in "Correlations of Random Binary Sequences
with Pre-Stated Operator Intention" and "The PEAR Proposition."

The findings hold profound implications regarding the nature of reality,
demonstrating that the physical world, including our physical bodies,
are secondary to a much larger *non-physical* reality system –
consciousness - which operates as an ***information system***.

Brittanica.com defines "information system" as "an integrated set of
components for collecting, storing, and processing data and for
providing information, knowledge, and digital products."

The 'Great Machine'

"The day science begins to study non-physical phenomena, it will make more progress in one decade than in all the previous centuries of its existence." – Nikola Tesla (1856-1943)

Highly influential but largely forgotten, Nikola Tesla is responsible for many of the electrical breakthroughs powering our lives, most notably for his role in the alternating-current (AC) electricity grid, which is still used to this day.

Bernard A. Behrend (1875-1932) was a respected contemporary of Tesla. *Clemson.edu* houses much of Behrend's works, describing his influence and achievements:

Behrend was a fellow of the American Institute of Electrical Engineers and served on a number of their committees, such as the Edison Medal Committee and the Electrical Machinery Committee (Chairman). Also, he was a Senior Vice-President of the Institute and was active on the Board of Directors. In addition, Behrend was a Fellow of the American Association for the Advancement of Science; the American Physical Society; the American Academy of Arts and Sciences; and a member of the American Society of Civil Engineers; the American Society of Mechanical Engineers; the Institute of Electrical Engineers (British); the Franklin Institute; and the Society for the Preservation of New England Antiquities. He was also a member of the Engineers Clubs in New York City and Boston, and the Athletic Club in Pittsburgh, Pennsylvania.

Mr. Behrend describes how Nikola Tesla changed the trajectory of technological achievement with his contributions:

*Suffice it to say that, were we to seize and to eliminate from our industrial world the results of Mr. Tesla's work, **the wheels of industry*** _would cease to turn, our electric cars and trains would stop, our towns would be dark, our mills would be dead and idle._ _Yea, so far reaching is this work, that it has become the warp and woof of industry..._ **His name marks an epoch in the advance of electrical science. From that work has sprung _a revolution in the electrical art._**

With funding secured from wealthy industrialist JP Morgan, Nikola Tesla began work on _Wardenclyffe Tower_, also known as _'Tesla Tower'_, in 1901.

(Wardenclyffe Tower)

Tesla's objective was to provide free and unlimited electrical power to _everyone_ in the world, using quantum technology well before quantum physics was an official branch of science.

Tesla outlines his vision in the February, 1901 edition of _Collier's Weekly_, in an article titled _'Talking with Planets'_:

Using the Earth itself as the medium for conducting the currents, thus dispensing with wires and all other artificial conductors... a machine which, to explain its operation in plain language, resembled a pump in its action, **drawing electricity from the Earth and driving it back into the same at an enormous rate, thus creating ripples or disturbances** *which, spreading through the Earth as through a wire, could be detected at great distances by carefully attuned receiving circuits. In this manner I was able to transmit to a distance, not only feeble effects for the purposes of signaling, but considerable amounts of energy, and later discoveries I made convinced me that **<u>I shall ultimately succeed in conveying power without wires, for industrial purposes, with high economy, and to any distance, however great</u>**.*

In a physical-based reality, concepts such as free-energy and levitation are absurd; in the quantum world, however, such anomalies are happenstance.

A 2017 article on *sciencedaily.com* titled *'Nanomagnets levitate thanks to quantum physics'* demonstrates that some things we think are impossible are only that way due to our lack of understanding:

*In collaboration with researchers from the Max Planck Institute for Quantum Optics, Munich, physicists in Oriol Romero-Isart's research group at the Institute for Theoretical Physics, Innsbruck University, and the Institute for Quantum Optics and Quantum Information, Austrian Academy of Sciences, have now shown that: "**<u>In the quantum world, tiny non-gyrating nanoparticles can stably levitate in a magnetic field.</u>**" "Quantum mechanical properties that are not noticeable in the macroscopic world but strongly influence nano objects are accountable for this phenomenon," says Oriol Romero-Isart.*

In 1903, JP Morgan halted funding and prevented completion of the *'Tesla Tower'*, crushing Tesla's dream of free-energy for the world. The structure was eventually torn down and **sold for scrap** prior to completion.

While Nikola Tesla's dream of free and unlimited energy for the world hasn't *yet* come to fruition, it is interesting to note his view regarding the '*system*' (in a 1937 article titled '*A Machine to End War*' on *PBS.org*):

<u>To me, the universe is simply a great machine which never came into being and never will end. The human being is no exception to the</u>

natural order. Man, like the universe, is a machine. Nothing enters our minds or determines our actions which is not directly or indirectly a response to stimuli beating upon our sense organs from without. Owing to the similarity of our construction and the sameness of our environment, we respond in like manner to similar stimuli, and from the concordance of our reactions, understanding is born.

Interestingly, Tesla's description of the universe as a *"great machine"* was also shared by physicist David Bohm (1917-1922).

Famousscientists.org describes Bohm: *"an American-born British quantum physicist who was a leading expert in the fields of theoretical physics, neuropsychology and philosophy. He is regarded as **one of the greatest and most influential theoretical physicists** of the 20th century."*

In his 1951 book *'Quantum Theory'*, Bohm also sees the universe as a big machine, though not *mechanical* in nature:

The entire universe must, on a very accurate level, be regarded as <u>a single indivisible unit</u> in which **separate parts appear as idealisations** *permissible only on a classical level of accuracy of description. This means that the view of the world being analogous to a **huge machine**, the predominant view from the sixteenth to nineteenth centuries, is now shown to be only approximately correct. **<u>The underlying structure of matter, however, is not mechanical.</u>** This means that the term "quantum mechanics" is very much a misnomer. It should, perhaps, be called "**<u>quantum nonmechanics</u>**".*

A *mechanical 'machine'* is similar to a *highly-organized self-aware information system* in many ways; **free will is the fundamental difference.**

Free Will

"God created things which had free will. That means creatures which can go wrong or right. Some people think they can imagine a creature which was free but had no possibility of going wrong, but I can't. If a thing is free to be good it's also free to be bad. And free will is what has made evil possible. Why, then, did God give them free will? **Because free will, though it makes evil possible, is also the only thing that makes possible any love or goodness or joy worth having.** <u>**A world of automata -of creatures that worked like machines- would hardly be worth creating.**</u> *The happiness which God designs for His higher creatures is the happiness of being freely, voluntarily united to Him and to each other in an ecstasy of love and delight compared with which the most rapturous love between a man and a woman on this earth is mere milk and water.* **And for that they've got to be free.***"*— C.S. Lewis, *'The Case for Christianity'*

Tom Campbell's *Big Theory of Everything* asserts that **free will is fundamental** to our virtual-reality simulation. This differs from the prevailing view within the natural, philosophical, and 'simulation' fields of science, which view reality as deterministic, or *completely* pre-destined.

A deterministic approach is built into much of the 'accepted' scientific and religious doctrines. In some religions, 'God' has already determined our path, and we are merely 'playing it out'. In 'accepted' science, an atom is borne at a certain speed and trajectory, following the 'laws' of relativity while traveling towards its pre-determined destiny; that humanity is a cluster of particles ultimately following a pre-determined, '*objective*' path.

A 2016 article from *thetlantic.com* titled *'There's No Such Thing as Free Will'* describes mainstream science's *opposition* to the concept of free will:

The sciences have grown steadily bolder in their claim that all human behavior can be explained through the clockwork laws of cause and effect. *This shift in perception is the continuation of an intellectual revolution that began about 150 years ago, when Charles Darwin first published On the Origin of Species.*

This deterministic approach operates with a *belief* that reality is following a physical pre-determined path (the article continues):

*In recent decades, research on the inner workings of the brain has helped to resolve the nature-nurture debate—**and has <u>dealt a further blow to the idea of free will.</u>** Brain scanners have enabled us to peer inside a living person's skull, revealing intricate networks of neurons and allowing scientists to reach broad agreement that these networks are shaped by both genes and environment.* **But there is also agreement in the scientific community that the <u>firing of neurons</u> determines not just some or most but <u>all of our thoughts, hopes, memories, and dreams.</u>**

The '*ancestor-simulation*' hypothesis, put forth by Oxford professor Nick Bostrom in '*Are You Living in a Computer Simulation?*', supposes that our current realty is a result of advanced humans running simulations of their past 'selves'.

The '*ancestor-simulation*' hypothesis also stems from a deterministic worldview, *believing* that the future has already occurred. **The hypothesis is built on a 'physical-universe' foundation**, dismissing consciousness as either not important or non-existent.

It is important to examine the utility, or usefulness, of competing concepts. Similar to the redundancy of the *'many worlds'* hypothesis, where new realities – or worlds - are continuously created for the smallest change in random variables, **what would be the point** of running an *'ancestor simulation'* on ourselves, or our former selves?

Besides expending the massive computing power required to run such a simulation, the majority of an *'ancestor simulation'* would be essentially pointless; time spent sleeping, bathroom breaks, and long hours at the office or in front of the television would all be played out – for essentially no reason whatsoever - since the future has already been determined.

What quantum mechanics clearly demonstrates, however, is that our physical reality is a 'virtual' piece of a much larger system, as David Bohm describes in his **1975** paper titled *'On the Intuitive Understanding of Nonlocality as Implied by Quantum Theory'*:

*We have reversed the usual classical notion that the independent "elementary parts" of the world are the fundamental reality, and that the various systems are merely particular contingent forms and arrangements of these parts. Rather, we say that **inseparable quantum interconnectedness of the whole universe is the fundamental reality, and that relatively independent behaving parts are merely particular and contingent forms within this whole.***

A *Big Theory of Everything* cannot account for just part of the picture, but must logically account for *everything*, including why free will is a *necessary* component of our shared virtual-reality *experience*.

Entropy

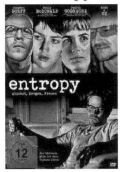

Merriam-webster.com broadly defines '*entropy*' as "*the degree of disorder or uncertainty in a system.*"

Entropy is an important aspect of thermodynamics, which is considered a 'fundamental' physical law of nature. *Entropy*, for example, is what causes an unused battery to lose its charge over time.

Google dictionary defines "*thermodynamics*" as "*the branch of **physical science** that deals with the relations between heat and other forms of energy (such as mechanical, electrical, or chemical energy), and, by extension, of the relationships between all forms of energy.*"

The *second law of thermodynamics* describes how physical systems *always* naturally increase their entropy, or disorder.

A 1999 article on *Boston University*'s physics website (*physics.bu.edu*) titled '*Entropy and the second law*' describes the attributes of entropy as it relates to thermodynamics:

The second law of thermodynamics is one of the most fundamental laws of nature, having profound implications. In essence, it says this:

55

The second law - **The level of disorder in the universe is steadily increasing. Systems tend to move from ordered behavior to more random behavior.**

One implication of the second law is that heat flows spontaneously from a hotter region to a cooler region, but will not flow spontaneously the other way. This applies to anything that flows: it will naturally flow downhill rather than uphill.

If you watched a film forwards and backwards, you would almost certainly be able to tell which way was which because of the way things happen. A pendulum will gradually lose energy and come to a stop, but it doesn't pick up energy spontaneously; an ice cube melts to form a puddle, but a puddle never spontaneously transforms itself into an ice cube; a glass falling off a table might shatter when it hits the ground, but the pieces will never spontaneously jump back together to form the glass again. Many processes are irreversible, and any irreversible process increases the level of disorder. One of the most important implications of the second law is that it indicates which way time goes - **time naturally flows in a way that increases disorder.**

The second law also predicts the end of the universe: <u>**it implies that the universe will end in a "heat death"**</u> **in which everything is at the same temperature. This is the ultimate level of disorder; if everything is at the same temperature, no work can be done, and** <u>**all the energy will end up as the random motion of atoms and molecules.**</u>

While considered a 'law' of nature, the *second law of thermodynamics* doesn't comply with quantum physics, however.

An article from *quantamagazine.org* titled '*The Quantum Thermodynamics Revolution*' demonstrates why a self-aware information system would logically work towards a lower-entropy state, instead of increasing entropy and degrading towards a "*heat death*":

Over time, however, as particles interact and become increasingly entangled, information about their individual states spreads and becomes shuffled and shared among more and more particles. Popescu and his colleagues believe that the arrow of **increasing <u>quantum entanglement underlies the expected rise in entropy</u>** — *the thermodynamic arrow of time. A cup of coffee cools to room temperature, they explain, because as coffee molecules collide with air molecules, the information that encodes their energy leaks out and is shared by the surrounding air.*

<u>*Understanding entropy as a subjective measure*</u> *<u>allows the universe as a whole to evolve without ever losing information</u>*. *Even as parts of the universe, such as coffee, engines and people, experience rising entropy as their quantum information dilutes, **the global entropy of the universe stays forever zero**.*

The *second law of thermodynamics* also does not comply with the basic building blocks of **all** living physical organisms: **cells.**

Scientists estimate that the human body contains **37.2 trillion** living cells. Instead of increasing entropy and moving towards disorder/chaos**, living cells actively work to reduce their entropy,** as *'the larger consciousness system'* also seeks to do.

A 2015 peer-reviewed study on *The National Center for Biotechnology Information*'s website (*ncbi.nlm.nih.gov*) titled *'Self-organization and entropy reduction in a living cell'* concludes that cells seek to lower their entropy and operate as "*biological computers*":

*The various points of reference regarding the nature of the living state undoubtedly reflect the prevailing Zeitgeist of the period in which a given theory has been created. The viewpoint of representing **the cell as a machine**, or even a factory, closely mirrors the worldview of the industrial revolution of the 19th century. Likewise, the currently popular opinion that **<u>living cells are intensely engaged in some type of computation</u>** is closely linked with the information technology revolution ushered into the second half of the 20th century as a result of the proliferation of computers in our daily lives. Both points of view have* *merits, i.e. the cell obeys the laws of physics such as the first law of thermodynamics and hence can be viewed as a thermodynamic machine and simultaneously* **it locally acts against the second law of thermodynamics by creating structural and functional order.** *In other words,* **it creates and maintains information by expending energy produced from nutrient** *in the form of ATP and GTP molecules. The latter aspect is thermodynamically analogous to the way a refrigerator works.* **However, a biological cell also processes information and engages in signaling thereby actively** <u>*performing computation*</u>**. It is safe to say that living cells can be viewed as both micro-factories (with nano-machines performing individual tasks), and** <u>**biological computers whose nano-chips**</u> *are the various proteins and peptides in addition to DNA and RNA. Most of the cell is what we could call hardware while a small fraction is* **analogous to computer software (for example the genetic code in the DNA that instructs for the synthesis of proteins).**

A *self-aware* information system – such as *'the larger consciousness system'* - would logically work to reduce its entropy/disorder, or in a broader sense it **would seek to improve itself in order to reduce inefficiencies and disorder – thereby actively preventing a *'heat death'*.**

A Chip off the Old Block

In Tom Campbell's *Big Theory of Everything* model, *'the larger consciousness system'* seeks to reduce its entropy by *splitting off*, or dividing into, multiple units; created *'in the image'* of *'the system'* itself.

Campbell refers to these units as *"individuated units of consciousness,"* or **IUOCs**.

IUOCs retain the *'likeness'* of consciousness, while being 'split off' from and contained within *'the larger consciousness system'*.

In *'My Big Toe: Discovery'*, Tom Campbell uses a 'bed-sheet' metaphor to describe how **IOUCs** are formed within *'the larger consciousness system'*:

Roughly analogous to a two-dimensional bed sheet that some children have stuck their hands into, pulling the sheet down around their wrists and forearms to make individuated hand puppets. ***Each hand puppet is an individual animated thing, and can interact with the other puppets*** *(by grabbing them perhaps). Yet for all their individuality (fat, thin, small, large, aggressive, calm), each hand puppet is part of the same sheet, existing only as protrusions in the sheet relative to flatter, more uniform parts of the sheet. The puppets exist as three-dimensional variations in the two-dimensional sheet. They are all part of the same sheet, but exist as* ***individual extensions of the two dimensional sheet into the third dimension****. It is worth noting that the extensions into the third dimension must be maintained by constraints. Imagine a rubber* *band that goes over the puppet and around the wrist of the child's hand. Remove the constraint and the sheet's protrusion into the third dimension quickly disappears. The sheet maintains its natural two dimensional existence unless some sort of constraint forces it to bulge in the third dimension.*

The process of 'splitting off' multiple *independent* units from within is consistent with cellular *"mitosis,"* which is described in a *National Institute of Health* (*ghr.nlm.nih.gov*) article titled '*How do cells divide?*':

Mitosis is a fundamental process for life. **During mitosis, _a cell_** **_duplicates all of its contents, including its chromosomes, and splits to_** **_form two identical daughter cells_**. *Because this process is so critical, the steps of mitosis are* **carefully controlled** *by a number of genes. When mitosis is not regulated correctly, health problems such as cancer can result.*

Quantum physicist David Bohm (1917-1992) describes the inherent connection between the *consciousness system* and the individual chunks that have been 'chipped off' from within.

We are all linked by a fabric of unseen connections. *This fabric is constantly changing and evolving.* **This field is directly structured and influenced by our behavior and by our understanding.**

While the **IUOC**s – 'split off' within '*the larger consciousness system*' - would be able to interact with other *IUOCs*, or cells, throughout '*the larger consciousness system*', the interactions would yield few meaningful results in an unregulated environment.

Tom Campbell compares *IOUCs* communicating with each other to a large chatroom, where growth – or *entropy reduction* – is difficult to achieve. In a large chatroom, unknown and often anonymous entities communicate in an unorganized manner. Actions have few consequences; some information may be beneficial and useful, but filtering out 'the noise' makes it redundant.

In order to ensure that the interactions yield more meaningful data/information, or reduce '*the larger consciousness system*'s entropy, the *IUOCs* split out, or divided (consistent with *cellular mitosis*) further, into what Campbell describes as '*Free Will Awareness Units*'.

Free Will Awareness Units

"Cogito, ergo sum" – Rene Descartes (commonly translated as *"I think, therefore I am"*)

Free Will Awareness Units, or *FWAUs*, as Tom Campbell outlines, allows for a more *personal* virtual experience.

The purpose of a *Free Will Awareness Unit* is to interact within a multitude of *virtual realities*, in order to gain experiences, make choices, and ultimately lower *the larger consciousness system*'s entropy, according to Campbell's *Big Theory of Everything* model.

This concept is further explored in a later chapter titled '*Experience Packets*'.

Reality Frames

ALTERED STATES

"Have you ever had a dream, Neo, that you were so sure was real? What if you were unable to wake from that dream? **How would you know the difference between the dream world and the real world**?*" –* Morpheus in *'The Matrix'*

In order to continually reduce its entropy, or disorder, *'the larger consciousness system'* has many simulations running simultaneously within itself, according to Campbell's *Big Theory of Everything*.

Dreams, for example, are a different virtual-reality state, with a different *rule set* and different consequences than our physical reality.

Some virtual realities are more constrained and others less, but all are virtual realities nonetheless.

In a dream, we can fall from the sky and suffer no damage, while in our physical reality we would splat onto the ground.

We imagine that our dreams are simply our imagination, and we scoff at the notion of *'out of body'* experiences and other phenomenon which have no apparent *physical* explanation, but they are all simply different *data streams.*

Near-Death Experiences

A 2015 article on *theatlantic.com* titled *''The Science of Near-Death Experiences'* describes the phenomenon, also referred to as *'NDE'*:

Though details and descriptions vary across cultures, the overall tenor of the experience is remarkably similar. Western near-death experiences are the most studied. Many of these stories relate the sensation of **floating up and viewing the scene around one's unconscious body; spending time in a beautiful, otherworldly realm; meeting spiritual beings (some call them angels) and a loving presence that some call God; encountering long-lost relatives or friends; recalling scenes from one's life; feeling a sense of connectedness to all creation as well as a sense of overwhelming, transcendent love; and finally being called, reluctantly, away from the magical realm and back into one's own body**. *Many NDErs report that their experience did not feel like a dream or a hallucination but was, as they often describe it,* **"more real than real life."** *They are profoundly changed afterward, and tend to have trouble fitting back into everyday life.*

Near-death experiences, dreams, and other 'altered states' are considered *'out-of-body'* experiences, demonstrating that consciousness transcends our physical reality frame, and that all reality frames and data streams we experience are 'virtual'.

Tom Campbell – on his website *my-big-toe.com* - reminds us that *'out-of-body'* isn't necessarily an accurate term, as you cannot get out of something that doesn't fundamentally exist:

It's not about the body; you are consciousness. That's what you are. Your consciousness is already out of your body. **You don't need to get out of your body; you just need to get into your consciousness.**

A 2014 article on *gizmodo.com* titled *'Scientists unlock mystery of out-of-body experiences (aka astral trips)'* describes a woman who is able to get *'out-of-body'* at will:

This is the very first time that this type of experience has been analyzed and documented scientifically. Researchers know that out-of-body experiences can be induced "by brain traumas, sensory deprivation, near-death experiences, dissociative and psychedelic drugs, dehydration, sleep, and electrical stimulation of the brain, among others. **It can also be deliberately induced by some.***" But this may be the first documented case of someone who can get into this state at will.*

The phenomenon is often dismissed as 'hallucinatory', since it lacks a 'physical' explanation.

The experience is 'real' to the experiencer, but since the experiencer never actually leaves their physical body, the mainstream conclusion is that there is *"no paranormal activity of any kind"* (the article continues):

So is it real or not?

It is real in the sense that she's actually experiencing it. The brain scans show that she's going through what she's claiming. But that doesn't mean that her "soul" is getting out of her body. **This is not an astral**

66

trip, like those described by mystics. <u>**There's no paranormal activity of any kind.**</u>

The fact is that, even while there aren't a lot of solid experiments on this subject except this research paper and a few others, scientists believe that these out-of-body experiences are a <u>***type of hallucination triggered by some neurological mechanism***</u>.

While the *mainstream* scientific consensus is that '*out-of-body*' experiences aren't 'real', those who have performed the *scientific* research have come to a much different conclusion.

Remote Viewing

Remote viewing is considered the act of intentionally getting '*out-of-body*'.

The *Princeton Engineering Anomalies Research* (**PEAR**) program, through scientific trials, found that the possibility that the remote viewing phenomenon is a *hallucination* is "**three parts in ten billion**."

The **PEAR** program researched "*remote perception*," popularly known as '*remote viewing*', demonstrating that the phenomenon is *scientifically correct* (found on the "*Experiments*" page of their archived website):

II. Remote Perception

*In another class of studies, the ability of human participants to **acquire information about spatially and temporally remote geographical targets, otherwise inaccessible by any of the usual sensory channels, has been thoroughly demonstrated over several hundred carefully conducted experiments**. The protocol required one participant, the "agent," to be stationed at a randomly selected location at a given time, and there to observe and record impressions of the details and ambiance of the scene. A second participant, the "percipient," located far from the scene and with no prior information about it, tried to sense its composition and character and to report these in a similar format to the agent's description.*

*Even casual comparison of the agent and percipient narratives produced in this body of experiments reveals **striking correspondences in both their general and specific aspects, indicative of some anomalous channel of information acquisition, well beyond any chance expectation**. Incisive analytical techniques have been developed and applied to these data to establish more precisely the quantity and quality of objective and subjective information acquired and to guide the* design of more effective experiments. **_Beyond confirming the validity of this anomalous mode of information acquisition, these analyses demonstrate that this capacity of human consciousness is also largely independent of the distance between the percipient and the target, and similarly independent of the time between the specification of the target and the perception effort._**

*Over its long history, PEAR has accumulated over **650 remote perception trials,** performed over several phases of investigation. Numerous scoring methods have involved various arrays of descriptor queries that have been addressed to both the physical targets and the percipients' subjective descriptions thereof, the responses to which have provided the basis for numerical evaluation and statistical assessment of the degree of anomalous information acquired under a variety of experimental protocols. Twenty-four such recipes were employed, with queries posed in binary, ternary, quaternary, and ten-level distributive formats. **_Thus treated, the composite database yields a probability against chance of approximately three parts in ten billion._**

Princeton University researchers have demonstrated that physical-matter is secondary to consciousness, but this information falls deafly on mainstream science's ears.

"Probability against chance of approximately three parts in ten billion" clearly demonstrates that *remote perception* is 'real', however does not serve as '*proof*' to a materialistic scientific establishment.

Proof is ultimately *subjective*, even for things which we accept as absolute fact.

Who's Your Daddy?

Many of us unequivocally know who our parents are, but the 'proof' is largely subjective.

Babymed.com describes the probability of a DNA test:

Every human cell contains a copy of the entire DNA of the person, 50% of

69

*it comes from the mother and 50% from the baby's father. Given the samples of at least the child and an alleged father, DNA paternity tests are held to be **99.999**% accurate.*

While 99.9999% accuracy is an extremely high level of certainty, the 'proof' of the result is subjective. Someone who sees that 'proof' as a forgery did not deem that information to be 'proof', demonstrating the subjectivity of *virtually* everything.

It is important to note that the DNA test is considered 'proof' in a court of law, though an *'out-of-body experience'*, with a *"probability against chance of approximately three parts in ten billion,"* is largely dismissed as *'hallucinatory'*.

This Virtual Life: Simulation Specifications

*"The soul, as an individuated unit of consciousness, is a subset of the larger consciousness, a constrained portion of nonphysical energy that contains enough memory and processing capability to support self-optimization through profitable intentional choice or free will. Your body is actually a virtual body, an experience of consciousness made apparently physical by constraining all interactions of the individuated limited awareness and experience to only **those allowed by the space-time rule-set**."* - Tom Campbell; *'My Big Toe: Discovery'*

'Physical-matter reality', or *PMR*, is how Tom Campbell describes the seemingly 'physical' reality which mainstream science accepts as fundamental.

Our *physical-matter reality* is a subset of *'the larger consciousness system'*, which hosts a multitude of different virtual reality fames, according to Tom Campbell's *Big Theory of Everything.*

It is important to note that all reality frames seem physical, or real, while we are interacting within them. For example, dreams feel physical, or real, when we are experiencing them.

Any data stream that we are immersed in is 'real', demonstrating that virtual-reality simulations are fundamentally physical in nature.

Similar to *The Sims*, our *physical-matter reality* is a virtual-reality *program* which follows certain principles, and abides by certain physical laws, or rules.

In a purely physical, *'objective'* reality, *randomness and disorder* would be the rule. But in our *physical-matter (virtual) reality*, the opposite holds true.

71

Self-organization

British mathematician Alan Turing (1912-1954), inventor of the *Turing machine*, wrote a paper in 1952 titled '*The Chemical Basis of Morphogenesis*'.

The paper outlines the physical process for which seemingly random bits of information, *or 'physical matter'*, 'spontaneously **self-organize'**. Instead of moving towards a state of disorder, or decay, as the *second law of thermodynamics* prescribes, *morphogenesis* demonstrates that matter *instinctively* seeks to lower its entropy through self-organization.

A 2014 article on *phys.org* titled '*A mathematical theory proposed by Alan Turing in 1952 can explain the formation of fingers*' describes Turing's contribution:

*His mathematical equations showed that starting from uniform condition (ie. a homogeneous distribution – no pattern) they could **spontaneously self-organise their concentrations into a repetitive spatial pattern**. This theory has come to be **accepted as an explanation of fairly simple patterns such as zebra stripes and even the ridges on sand dunes, but in embryology it has been resisted for decades as an explanation of how structures such as fingers are formed.***

In order for random matter to spontaneously organize, there must be a *fundamental* underlying 'code' in its architecture.

The Code

*"[The universe] cannot be read until we have learnt the language and become familiar with the characters in which it is written. **It is written in mathematical language**, and the letters are triangles, circles and other geometrical figures, without which means it is humanly impossible to comprehend a single word."* – Galileo Galilei (1564 – 1642)

Theoretical physicist Jim Gates, who served on former US President Barack Obama's *Council of Advisors on Science and Technology*, is a leading researcher on 'string-theory' related phenomena, and has made 'strange' discoveries with *adinkras.*

Adinkras are graphical representations of sets of equations based on the code which underlies physical reality, also referred to as *supersymmetry*.

At the 10th annual *'Isaac Asimov Theory of Everything'* conference in 2011, available on *Youtube.com*, Gates describes the bizarre nature of *adinkras* in an exchange with host Neil Degrasse Tyson:

*Gates: "You find that **buried in them are computer codes just like the type you find in a browser**, when you go and search the web. I'm left with the puzzle of trying to figure out whether I live in the matrix or not."*

*Degrasse Tyson: "Are you saying your attempt to understand the <u>**fundamental operations of nature**</u> lead you to a set of equations that are indistinguishable from the equations that drive search engines and browsers on our computers?"*

*Gates: "<u>**That is correct.**</u>"*

Degrasse Tyson: "So you're saying, as you dig deeper you find computer code writ in the fabric of the cosmos?"

*Gates: "**Into the equations that we once used to describe the cosmos, yes... <u>Computer code; strings of bits of ones and zeroes.</u>**"*

Degrasse Tyson: "It's not just sort of resembles computer code; you're saying it is computer code?"

*Gates: "<u>**It's not even just 'is' computer code; it's a special kind of computer code that was invented by a scientist named Claude Shannon in the 1940s. That's what we find buried very deeply inside the equations that occur in string theory, and in general in systems that we say are 'super-symmetric'.**</u>"*

The "*computer code*" is evident in natural processes, such as snowflakes and honeycombs:

'The code' causes birds to fly *in-formation:*

'The code' is what causes **all** circles to have the same ratio, known as Pi.

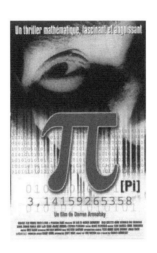

'The code' is at the core of **all** of the *processes* in our *physical-matter reality*.

The Golden Ratio

Snail shells, pinecones, and ocean waves are a few ways in which nature exhibits 'the golden ratio'.

A 2015 article on *Mother Nature's Network* (*mnn.com*) titled '*How the golden ratio manifests in nature*' describes the *simple* mathematical formula behind much of nature's vast complexity:

*The golden ratio (often represented by the Greek letter φ) is directly tied to a numerical pattern known as the Fibonacci sequence, which is a list composed of numbers that are the sum of the previous two numbers in the sequence. Often referred to as the natural numbering system of the cosmos, the Fibonacci sequence starts out simply (0+1= **1**, 1+1=**2**, 1+2=**3**, 2+3=**5**, 3+5=**8**...), but before long, you'll find yourself adding up numbers in the thousands and millions (10946+17711=**28657**, 17711+28657=**46368**, 28657+46368=**75025**...) and it just keeps going on forever like that.*

When a Fibonacci number is divided by the Fibonacci number that came before it, it approaches the golden ratio, which is an irrational number that starts out as 1.6180339887... and, once again, goes on forever.

Fractals

"Where there is matter, there is geometry." — Johannes Kepler (1571-1630)

Fractals are an expression of *'the code'*.

Dictionary.com provides a scientific definition of *"fractal"* :

A complex geometric pattern exhibiting self-similarity in that small details of its structure viewed at any scale repeat elements of the overall pattern. *See more at chaos.*

Our Living Language : Fractals are often associated with **recursive operations** *on shapes or sets of numbers, in which* **the result of the operation is used as the input to the <u>same operation</u>, repeating the process indefinitely. The operations themselves are usually very simple**, *but the resulting shapes or sets are often* **<u>dramatic and complex</u>**, *with interesting properties.*

Benoit Mandelbrot (1924-2010) is considered the *'father of fractals'*. A 2017 article on *theatlantic.com* titled *'Why Fractals Are So Soothing'* reveals how fractals are the self-replicating building blocks of our *physical-matter reality*:

Benoit Mandelbrot first coined the term 'fractal' in 1975, discovering that simple mathematic rules apply to a vast array of things that looked visually complex or chaotic. **As he proved, fractal patterns were often found in nature's roughness—in clouds, coastlines, plant leaves, ocean waves, the rise and fall of the Nile River, and in the clustering of galaxies.** *To understand fractal patterns at different scales, picture a trunk of a tree and a branch: they might contain the same angles as that same branch and a smaller branch, as well as the converging veins of the leaf on that branch. And so on.* **You can have fractals creating what looks like chaos.**

Modern science is still looking to 'catch-up' on their understanding of the fractal nature of our reality.

A 2009 *NOVA* special took a closer look at the **still** little-understood subject. The special, titled *'Fractals: Hunting the Hidden Dimension'*, is outlined on *pbs.org*:

*Mysteriously beautiful fractals are **shaking up the world** of mathematics and deepening our understanding of **nature.***

*You may not know it, but fractals, like the air you breathe, are all around you. Their irregular, repeating shapes are found in **cloud formations and tree limbs, in stalks of broccoli and craggy mountain ranges, even in the rhythm of the human heart**. In this film, NOVA takes viewers on a fascinating quest with a group of maverick mathematicians determined to decipher the rules that govern fractal geometry.*

*For centuries, fractal-like irregular shapes were considered **beyond the boundaries of mathematical understanding**. Now, mathematicians have **finally begun** mapping this uncharted territory. Their remarkable findings are deepening our understanding of nature and **stimulating a new wave of scientific, medical, and artistic innovation** stretching from the ecology of the rain forest to fashion design. The documentary highlights a host of filmmakers, fashion designers, physicians, and researchers who are using fractal geometry to innovate and inspire.*

Fractals are the self-replicating building blocks which make up our *physical-matter reality*, and presumably the *data-dispersion* and replication logic employed by '*the larger consciousness system*'.

Tom Campbell describes these adaptive fractals as '*process fractals*'. In '*My Big Toe: Inner Workings*', Campbell outlines the concept:

*To be sure, the Fundamental Process does not generate a geometric fractal; instead, it produces a **process fractal**. You may need to generalize your concept of fractals, but the similarity to fractal dynamics and structure is obvious. When we look at our reality and at the process of evolution that built it, we see **one simple process repeated at various scales and levels generating intricate convoluted process patterns. We see the digital (virtual) energy of synergistic organization creating a complex ecosystem that employs the Fundamental Process to recursively iterate layer after layer of interactive process**. Each layer becomes the foundation for the next. Together, consciousness and the*

Fundamental Process evolve an ever growing, monstrously complex reality system – *a system where every part or entity at every level of existence explores its full potential while populating only those states determined by itself (often using criteria germane to the next higher-level) to be significant and useful to itself (often for a higher-level purpose or activity). Solar systems, galaxies, human bodies, insects, and consciousness all evolve through the same pattern.*

Order from Chaos

(***Ordo Ab Chao*** - Masonic emblem - as defined by *masonicdictionary.com*: *A Latin expression, meaning Order out of Chaos.*)

Chaos theory demonstrates that while there are physical laws of nature, **the future remains uncertain.**

An article on *philosophynow.org* titled '*Chaos & An Unpredictable Tomorrow*' describes this phenomenon:

*Chaos theory suggests that the behavior of **complex systems can follow laws and yet their <u>future states remain in principle unpredictable</u>.** The behavior of complex systems is exquisitely sensitive to conditions, so that small changes at the start can result in ever larger changes over time. Hence, chaos theory implies that **<u>the future is not predictable based on past events</u>**, as it used to be thought to be. Or in words that have been attributed to both physicist Niels Bohr and baseball manager Yogi Berra, "Prediction is very difficult, especially about the future."*

Classical physics posits that physical processes are completely predictable, and therefore the future is deterministic; while *chaos theory* demonstrates the flaw in that *philosophical* logic (the article continues):

All of this raises a most interesting question: **Do we need to rethink our notions not only of the future, but of who we are? To the extent that we identify with our consciousness, this seems to mean that <u>each of us is more intimately connected with the world than we ordinarily imagine.</u>** *But like other complex dynamic systems,* **what we are is unbounded** *– even if we can be distinguished from other things for many purposes, such as death, taxes, and marriage. Whether we see our connection to the universe as a whole as metaphysically spooky depends on whether (as in the tale of the blind monks) we characterize the elephant by feeling its individual parts; or instead we see that the parts have arisen in relationship to each other and to the greater environment as a whole, and so can identify the whole thing.*

Clearly, chaos theory has uncovered **powerful natural processes that we're only beginning to understand.** *So, what are we to conclude about the future? Given chaos theory's contention that complex systems act deterministically but are* **not thereby predictable***, we can say that soothsayers and all such pundits are overpaid! But to be serious,* **there is a sense in which the future is open.** *Since complex systems are extremely sensitive to initial conditions,* **to circular feedback, and to interactions with other complex systems, what is going to happen in the world seems to depend on how all the world's complex systems behave from moment to moment.** <u>**The future, then, is self-organized, but to no particular end, purpose, or plan.**</u>

The Butterfly Effect

The *'butterfly effect'* demonstrates that small changes within an interconnected information system can have a profound *downstream* effect.

Dictionary.com defines "*butterfly effect*" as "t*he idea, used in chaos theory, that a very small difference in the initial state of a physical system can make a significant difference to the state at some later time.*"

The *'butterfly effect'* demonstrates why future events, such as weather patterns, can be difficult or even *impossible* to predict.

An *MIT Technology Review* article (on *technologyreview.com*) titled *'When the Butterfly Effect Took Flight'* outlines the phenomenon:

On a winter day 50 years ago, Edward Lorenz, SM '43, ScD '48, a mild-mannered meteorology professor at MIT, entered some numbers into a computer program simulating weather patterns and then left his office to get a cup of coffee while the machine ran. When he returned, he noticed a result that would change the course of science.

*The computer model was based on 12 variables, representing things like temperature and wind speed, whose values could be depicted on graphs as lines rising and falling over time. On this day, Lorenz was repeating a simulation he'd run earlier—but he had rounded off one variable from .506127 to .506. To his surprise, **that tiny alteration drastically transformed the whole pattern** his program produced, over two months of simulated weather.*

The '*butterfly effect*' can also predict how small decisions within our daily lives determine how our future will *play* out.

In an *abcnews.com* article titled '*Science Behind The Butterfly Effect*', small day to day actions are shown to cumulatively determine the course of our lives:

Mathematician John Murray and psychologist John Gottman examined 700 couples for over a decade. They recorded conversations early in each marriage and marked how many times they smiled, joked, raised their eyebrows or mocked each other. Then, using a set of equations based on a branch of math related to chaos theory, Murray estimated how long each couple would remain married.

"One equation incorporates how the wife will speak, depending on what the husband says, what her state of mind was before and so on. Then you have the equivalent equation of the husband. These two equations can generate chaotic solutions," Murray explained.

*Using the equations, Murray said they **predicted the success of each marriage 94 percent of the time.***

Our *physical-matter reality* is governed by probabilities, and our choices ultimately determine the trajectory of our lives.

The *Quantum* Computer

*"All observed phenomena are consistent with the model in which **the universe is a quantum computer,** e.g., a **quantum cellular automaton**. The quantum computational model of the universe explains previously unexplained features, most importantly, the co-existence in the universe of randomness and order, and of simplicity and complexity."* – MIT Professor Seth Lloyd; author of 2016 paper '*The Universe as Quantum Computer*')

A reality based on "*computer code*" and governed by self-organization and mathematics must *somehow* be calculated, and only a certain type of *computer system* can handle such a task.

To understand the nature of our *physical-matter reality*, it is important to understand the nature of *quantum computing*.

IBM understands the importance of quantum computing and its relation to the physical world. On *ibm.com* they address the question: "*How do quantum computers work?'*:

*Classical computers encode information in bits. Each bit can take the value of 1 or 0. These 1s and 0s act as on/off switches that ultimately drive computer functions. Quantum computers, on the other hand, are based on qubits, which operate according to two key principles of quantum physics: **superposition and entanglement. Superposition means that each qubit can represent both a 1 and a 0 at the same time. Entanglement means that qubits in a superposition can be correlated with each other; that is, the state of one (whether it is a 1 or a 0) can depend on the state of another.** Using these two principles, qubits can act as **more sophisticated** switches, enabling quantum computers to function in ways that allow them to solve difficult problems that are __intractable using today's computers.__*

Quantum computing is not just different in its methodology, it also requires vastly more computing power than present technology allows.

On *ibm.com*, a section titled '*A Beginner's Guide to Quantum Computing*' describes how current quantum computing technology cannot accurately calculate *a cup of coffee*:

Nature -- *including molecules like caffeine* -- **follows the laws of quantum mechanics**, *a branch of physics that explores* **how the physical world works at the most fundamental levels**. *At this level, particles behave in* **strange ways, taking on more than one state at the same time, and interacting with other particles that are very far away**. *Quantum computing harnesses these quantum phenomena to process information in a novel and promising way.*

The computers we use today are known as classical computers. They've been a driving force in the world for decades -- advancing everything from healthcare to how we shop. But there are certain problems that classical computers will simply never be able to solve. Consider the caffeine molecule in a cup of coffee. **Surprisingly,** **it's complex enough that no computer that exists or could be built would be capable of modeling caffeine and fully understanding its detailed structure and properties. This is the type of challenge quantum has the potential to tackle.**

Instead of wasting computing power, or resources, calculating every molecule at every point in time, a quantum computer only calculates, or **renders information**, when required.

Instead of a pre-determined result based on prior physical processes, our *physical-matter reality* is based on *probability*. When a measurement is being taken by a conscious observer, '*the larger consciousness system*' renders a result based on the '*probability distribution of the possibilities*', as Tom Campbell describes.

Tom Campbell and three additional physicists outline these phenomena in peer-reviewed paper published on *International Journal of Quantum Foundations* (*ijqf.org*), titled '*On testing the simulation hypothesis*':

Abstract

Can the hypothesis that reality is a simulation be tested? We investigate this question based on the assumption that if the system performing the simulation is finite (i.e. has limited resources), then to achieve low computational complexity, such a system would, as in a video game, **render content (reality) only at the moment that information becomes available for observation by a player and not at the moment of detection by a machine** *(that would be part of the simulation and whose Detection would also be part of the internal computation performed by the Virtual Reality server before rendering content to the player). Guided by this principle we describe conceptual wave/particle duality experiments aimed at testing the simulation hypothesis.*

Introduction

Wheeler advocated [42] that "Quantum Physics requires a new view of reality" integrating physics with digital (quanta) information. Two such views emerge from the presupposition that reality could be computed. The first one, which includes Digital Physics [46] and the cellular automaton interpretation of Quantum Mechanics [35], proposes that the universe is the computer. The second one, which includes the simulation hypothesis [7, 9, 43], suggests that **the observable reality is entirely virtual and the system performing the simulation (the computer) is distinct from its simulation** *(the universe). In this*

paper we investigate the possibility of experimentally testing the second view and base our analysis on the assumption that the system performing the simulation has limited computational resources. **Such a system would therefore use computational complexity as a minimization/selection principle for algorithm design.**

The paper continues to describe how the quantum computer *calculating* our reality, consistent with virtual-reality video games, only computes and renders results when necessary:

On Rendering Reality

It is now well understood in the emerging science of Uncertainty Quantification [15] that low complexity computation must be performed with hierarchies of multi-fidelity models [13]. It is also now well understood, in the domain of game development, **that low computational complexity requires rendering/displaying content** <u>**only when observed by a player**</u>*. Recent games, such as No-Man's Sky and Boundless, have shown that vast open universes (potentially including "over 18 quintillion planets with their own sets of flora and fauna"* **by creating content, only at the moment the corresponding information becomes available for observation by a player, through randomized generation techniques** *(such as procedural generation). Therefore,* **to minimize computational complexity in the simulation hypothesis,** <u>**the system performing the simulation would render reality only at the moment the corresponding information becomes available for observation by a conscious observer (a player), and the resolution/granularity of the rendering would be adjusted to the level of perception of the observer.**</u> *More precisely, using such techniques,* **the complexity of simulation would not be constrained by the apparent size of the universe or an underlying pre-determined mesh/grid size but by the number of players and the resolution of the information made available for observation.**

Virtual-reality games such as *The Sims* rely on classical computing and manual programming to create a semi-realistic simulation.

'The larger consciousness system', operating as a highly-powerful quantum computer, allows reality to evolve, avoiding unnecessary micro-calculations for every possible molecular change.

The *quantum program* only renders results, or makes calculations, when a measurement is taken by a player. This *Schrödinger's cat*-like approach ensures that processing power is only expelled on an as-needed basis, conserving energy and increasing *the larger consciousness system's* probability of survival.

The Rules

*"**No one knows who wrote the laws of physics or where they come from**. Science is based on testable, reproducible evidence, and so far we cannot test the universe before the Big Bang."* – Physicist and author Michio Kaku

Tools within *the game* are used to measure attributes and truths within the game, but **the source of *the game* cannot be measured, and does not reveal itself in the language of *the game* itself.**

In a computed virtual reality, there must be rules. Without rules, there would be no structure.

Classical physics serves to essentially define and outline the *rule set* of our *physical-matter reality*.

In our *physical-matter reality*, speed cannot exceed the *'speed of light'*, demonstrating a well-defined rule.

Classical physics can calculate the speed of light, but has no explanation for the cause.

In *The Sims*, the speed that light travels from one pixel to the next according to the game's rule set.

When you turn on a flashlight in our *physical-matter reality*, the same rules apply.

The *rule set* provides parameters and keeps the simulation consistent and *orderly*.

The *rule set* governing *physical-matter reality* is tight, providing real-time feedback and consequences; the rule set governing our dreams is much looser, allowing us to fly and providing few *virtual-consequences* for our actions.

'*Sparc*', a *Sony PlayStation* virtual-reality video game, demonstrates how rule sets are established and applied within virtual-reality simulations.

On the FAQ page of their website *playsparc.com*, the details of the game are outlined:

Sparc is a virtual sport, or vSport - a unique physical sport only possible in virtual reality, in which players compete in full-body VR gameplay and connect in an online community.

What is VR?

*We believe that Virtual reality, or VR, is the future of interactive entertainment. **VR offers the simulation of real** or fictional environments using specialised wearable **computer hardware to give users the illusion of being in another world. Core to the virtual reality experience is complete user immersion**, including 360-degree visuals generated by a head-mounted display.*

What is a vSport?

*A vSport is a physical sport not possible in the real world – **a unique full-body experience that can only be delivered through virtual reality, with a well-defined rule-set** and physicality as found in real-world sports. In Sparc, your VR hardware is your sporting equipment. We've designed Sparc so that **players can express and improve their skill through their physical actions so when you play, it's really you** - **not a fictional character in a fictional world.***

Digital-video, like *motion pictures* and virtual-reality video games, string individual frames together to create movement, or motion.

Like a virtual-reality video game, our computed *physical-matter reality* is made up of discrete bits of information, and those bits are strung together to create constant and continuous motion.

Planck's length, developed by *Nobel Prize* winning physicist Max Planck, is the smallest scale in which the principles of classical physics apply, seemingly measuring the size of each *pixel* within our *physical-matter reality*.

Tom Campbell, in *'My Big TOE: Awakening'*, outlines *Planck's length:*

*Planck's length (16x10 - 36 m) – a measure of the point at which some of the world's best physicists say that **our 3D space becomes granular (is composed of <u>non - continuous discrete cells</u>)** .*

Time

*"Of all obstacles to a thoroughly penetrating account of existence, none looms up more dismayingly than "time." **Explain time? Not without explaining existence. Explain existence? Not without explaining time.** To uncover the deep and hidden connection between time and existence, to close on itself our quartet of questions, is a task for the future."* - Physicist John Archibald Wheeler_(1911-2008)

Time is fundamental within our *physical-matter virtual reality*. For a digital simulation to progress, time is necessary. Within our *physical-matter reality simulation*, time operates in a linear fashion - progressing one *Planck length,* or *Delta T*, at a time.

In '*My Big TOE: Awakening*', Tom Campbell demonstrates that the concept of **time is fundamental** to a digital virtual-reality simulation:

Time is a technology*, a construct of a self-modifying evolving* *consciousness, an artifact of a system of energy improving its internal organization. When the potential energy of primordial consciousness (the potential to self-organize more profitably) evolves the ability to decrease its own entropy one infinitesimal smidgen,* **time is the byproduct of that internal change.** **_Time separates the "before" state from the "after" state._** **Change creates the notion of time. Awareness of change necessitates the idea of a personal time.**

Mainstream science, on the other hand, *believes* that '*time is an illusion*'. In an objective, physical-only world that began with an explosion of physical matter, everything is pre-determined, making time irrelevant, and technically non-existent.

A *newscientist.com* article titled '***Saving time: Physics killed it. Do we need it back?***' outlines the *materialis/objective* worldview regarding time:

IMAGINE standing outside the universe. Not just outside space, but outside time too. From this spectacular vantage point, you gaze down upon the universe. At one end you see its beginning: the big bang. At the other, you see… whatever it is that happens there. Somewhere in the middle is you, a minuscule worm: at one end a baby, the other end a corpse. From this impossible perspective, time does not flow, and there is no "now". **Time is static. Immutable. Frozen.**

Fantastical as it seems, **_for most physicists today the universe is just like that_**. *We might think of time flowing from a real past into a not-yet-real future, but our current theories of space and time teach us that past, present and future are all equally real –* **and fundamentally indistinguishable.** **_Any sense that our "now" is somehow special, or that time flows past it, is an illusion we create in our heads._**

Probability Distribution

*"The only thing that can accurately describe an elementary particle is a **probability function** that, in itself, **contains nothing about the quality of being or the physical existence of that particle**."* – Physicist Werner Heisenberg (1932 *Nobel Prize* winner)

In a simulation with a well-defined rule set, *'probability distribution'* determines likely outcomes for any and all scenarios.

Investopedia.com defines *'probability distribution'* as *"a statistical function that describes **all the possible values and likelihoods that a random variable can take within a given range.** This range will be between the minimum and maximum statistically possible values, but where the possible value is likely to be plotted on the probability distribution depends on a number of factors. These factors include the distribution's mean, standard deviation, skewness and kurtosis."*

Columbia University professor and physicist Brian Greene, in his 1999 book *'The Elegant Universe'*, describes how the nature of our reality is *probabilistic*, and not deterministic/objective:

*Just a few months after de Broglie's suggestion, Schrödinger took the decisive step... by determining an equation that governs the shape and the **evolution of probability waves**, or as they became known, wave functions. It was not long before Schrödinger's equation and **the probabilistic interpretation were being used to make wonderfully accurate predictions**. By 1927, <u>therefore,</u> classical <u>innocence had been lost. Gone were the days of a</u> clockwork universe <u>whose individual constituents were set in motion at some moment in the past and obediently fulfilled their inescapable, uniquely determined destiny</u>. According to quantum mechanics, the universe evolves according to a rigorous and **precise mathematical formalism, but this framework determines only the probability that any particular function will happen**—<u>**not which future actually ensues.**</u>*

Marcus du Sautoy, in his book *'The Great Unknown: Seven Journeys to the Frontiers of Science',* reaffirms the probabilistic nature of our *physical-matter reality*:

*One of the most curious consequences of quantum physics is that a particle like an electron can seemingly be in more than one place at the same time until it is observed, at which point there seems to be **a random choice** made about where the particle is really located. Scientists currently believe that this randomness is genuine, not just caused by a lack of information. Repeat the experiment under the same conditions **and you may get a different answer each time.***

Any time we take a measurement, we force a *'random draw from the probability distribution of the possibilities'*, as Thomas Campbell describes, forcing *'the larger consciousness system'* to *render* a result based on the mathematical probabilities of any given scenario.

Psi Uncertainty

In order for a virtual-reality simulations to be effective, it must maintain its authenticity.

In '*My Big TOE: Awakening*', Tom Campbell defines the '*psi uncertainty principle*':

*The psi uncertainty principle makes the scientific objective measurement of psi performance problematical, but only from the PMR (**Stith**: physical-matter reality) perspective. As soon as there are outside observers to report and measure the miracles (reduce the uncertainty about reported violations of traditional PMR physics), **the miracles diminish** - and insiders cannot be trusted to be objective and therefore cannot be believed {and therefore can be discounted}.*

Let's explore how the randomness of certain natural events is related to the psi uncertainty principle. A focused and directed consciousness (physically embodied or not) may take advantage of the uncertainty or randomness in physical interactions, situations, or phenomena by subtly applying psycho-kinetics (PK) or telepathic suggestion to manipulate events toward a particular outcome. The results of these manipulations would **simply appear within PMR to be good or bad luck, an intuitive bolt out of the blue, or a random skewing of the expected statistical distribution**. Such manipulations are typically helpful and relatively common. **They created no contradictions and pose no causality problems within PMR {widespread loss of belief in PMR as a physically objective reality} as long as there is enough uncertainty (lack of objective proof) to hide the paranormal outside influence and satisfy the psi uncertainty principle.**

The Game

*"Here some one thrust these cards into these old hands of mine, swears that I must play them, and no others. And damn me, Ahab, but thou actest right, **live in the game, and die in it**."* – Herman Melville (1819-1891; from *Moby Dick*)

Modeling reality as a game, or simulation, has been an effective strategy for thousands of years.

In the 5th B.C., the ancient Greeks are credited with inventing *'petteia'*, which is generally accepted as the first well-documented *'wargame'*.

Boardgamegeek.com provides background on the ancient *game* of *'petteia'*:

*Roughly translated as '**Robbers**', this abstract battle game was known to be played by the Romans, and versions of the same game may well have been played before by the Ancient Greeks and Egyptians, and afterwards by the Persians. Games archaeologists and historians disagree hotly* about just about every aspect of this game: board size, number and distribution of playing pieces, use of a king piece, age, priority, etc, etc; the list goes on. However, there is evidence that the game existed, both in literature and in archaeological finds. All this disagreement suggests that, **as the game traveled out to the far flung regions of empire, it was altered and developed by gamers and gamblers.**

The Foreign Policy Group, claiming that they reach *"an international audience of millions and has become a trusted source of insight and analysis for leaders from government, business, finance, and the academic world,"* applies gaming-logic to real-world events to predict – *and assist with determining* – outcomes.

On their website *foriegnpolicy.com*, an article titled *'War Games: A Short History'* outlines the history and importance of *'wargames'*:

Ever since the first warrior picked up a wooden stick in imitation of a sword, the line between war and entertainment has been decidedly blurry. Military training in ancient Greece and chivalric Europe gave rise to the Olympics and medieval jousting tournaments; paintball guns and **<u>video games</u>** *have become tools for honing the skills of today's soldiers.* **The realm of strategy, however, is where games have exerted the most remarkable impact on the conduct of war, serving as a tool for, as one U.S. Army general put it, <u>"writing history in advance."</u>**

Dictionary.com defines *"war game"* as *"a simulated military operation, carried out to test the validity of a war plan or operational concept: in its simplest form, two opposing teams of officers take part, and when necessary, military units of the required strength are employed."*

War games are often viewed as military-only simulations, though their scope also encompasses *any and all* political and social factors relevant to *the game.*

Founded in 1948, the *RAND Corporation* is one of the world's most influential *'think tanks'*, working closely with governments and private-organizations.

On their website, *rand.org*, they outline the importance of 'Wargaming':

*Wargames are analytic games that simulate aspects of warfare at the tactical, operational, or strategic level. They are used to examine warfighting concepts, train and educate commanders and analysts, explore scenarios, and assess how force planning and posture choices affect campaign outcomes. **RAND has developed and can execute various types of wargames, including scenario exercises, tabletop map exercises, "Day After..." games, and computer-supported exercises.***

The approach of viewing reality as a game is known as *"game theory,"* defined by *dictionary.com* as *"a mathematical theory that deals with strategies for maximizing gains and minimizing losses within **prescribed constraints, as the rules of a card game**: widely applied in the solution of various decision-making problems, **as those of military strategy and business policy.**"*

Game theory demonstrates that reality is often best understood as ***a game.***

A 2013 article on *popsci.com* titled '*Why I Let My Students Cheat On Their Game Theory Exam*' outlines this *philosophical* approach:

*Much of evolution and natural selection can be summarized in three short words: "**Life is games.**" In any game, the object is to win—be that defined as leaving the most genes in the next generation, getting the best grade on a midterm, or successfully inculcating critical thinking into your students. **An entire field of study, Game Theory, is devoted to mathematically describing the games that nature plays. Games can determine why ant colonies do what they do, how viruses evolve to exploit hosts, or how human societies organize and function.***

Society at-large is beginning to recognize that simulations, as an expression of *game theory*, provide more meaningful results than most traditional methods.

A 2016 *Harvard Business Review (hbr.org)* article titled *'How Companies Are Using Simulations, Competitions, and Analytics to Hire'* describes how simulations are beginning to become recognized as an integral part of business:

*Increasingly (but sporadically at best), one of us has been asked to judge a potential CEO's capacity to perform on the basis of a simulation which mimics the type of challenges a potential CEO will face. One such executive is Alan Mulally, whose test results (among some of the best we've ever seen) were highly predictive of his successes at Boeing and as CEO of Ford. At Humana, Korn Ferry used case simulations prior to recommending Bruce Broussard as CEO. Mike McCallister, the outgoing CEO at the time, told us, "When selecting a CEO successor, the Board and I wanted a window on how a candidate would respond to different challenges and **the simulation case gave us hard data beyond the interviews alone**." Broussard's successful performance as CEO closely approximated the predictions. This is a big step forward in assessing candidates beyond interviews and resumes, and though important, referencing also often fails to be predictive. Of course, companies must have a **clear sense of their strategy** and what types of leadership challenges are most likely in order for a simulation to be valid and realistic.*

Recognizing the importance and benefit of simulations, *'the larger consciousness system'* had the means and motive to create virtual realities to further its goal of reducing entropy.

The Nash Equilibrium

1994 *Nobel Prize* winner John Nash - profiled in the 2001 movie '*A Beautiful Mind*' – was an important contributor to *game theory*.

His most notable contribution, the *Nash equilibrium*, applies mathematical formulas to real-world situations – with *surprising* accuracy.

A 2016 *economist.com* article titled '*What is the Nash equilibrium and why does it matter?*' outlines the concept:

The Nash equilibrium helps economists understand how decisions that are good for the individual can be terrible for the group. *This tragedy of the commons explains why we overfish the seas, and why we emit too much carbon into the atmosphere. Everyone would be better off if only we could agree to show some restraint.* **But given what everyone else is doing, fishing or gas-guzzling makes individual sense.** *As well as explaining doom and gloom, it also helps policymakers come up with solutions to tricky problems. Armed with the Nash equilibrium, economics geeks claim to have raised billions for the public purse. In 2000 the British government used their help to design a special auction*

that sold off its 3G mobile-telecoms operating licences for a cool £22.5 billion ($35.4 billion). Their trick was to **treat the auction as a game**, *and tweak the rules so that the best strategy for bidders was to make bullish bids (the winning bidders were less than pleased with the outcome).*
Today the Nash equilibrium underpins modern microeconomics *(though with some refinements). Given that it promises economists the power to pick winners and losers, it is easy to see why.*

'Snitches Get Stitches'

"The hazards of the generalized prisoner's dilemma are removed by the match between the right and the good." – John Rawls

The *'prisoner's dilemma'* is a key component of *'game theory'*, demonstrating that selfish decisions often produce a negative outcome for all parties involved.

Investopedia.com defines *"prisoner's dilemma"* as *"a paradox in decision analysis in which **two individuals acting in their own self-interest pursue a course of action that does not result in the ideal outcome**. The typical prisoner's dilemma is set up in such a way that both parties choose to protect themselves at the expense of the other participant. As a result of following a purely logical thought process, both participants find themselves in a worse state than if they had cooperated with each other in the decision-making process."*

The Player

*"Experience requires interaction. To make that interaction more effective a simpler constrained environment is needed – our local physical reality is an elementary school – **a virtual reality learning lab for individuated units of budding consciousness.**"* – Tom Campbell (lecture slide)

Our *physical-matter reality* is a highly-evolved simulation with a tight rule-set, offering countless opportunities for entropy-reduction.

For our *physical-matter reality* simulation to be meaningful, **players are required.**

A *'free will awareness unit'*, created by an *'individuated unit of consciousness'* with the goal of reducing entropy, or disorder, within *'the larger consciousness system'*, **hosts an avatar** within this physical simulation, in Thomas Campbell's *Big Theory of Everything* model.

In our *physical-matter reality*, we cannot 'pause' the game, or switch avatars at will.

All avatars are not created equally, accounting for certain restraints in our physical lives.

An avatar with one arm has different physical constraints than an avatar with both arms; a blind avatar faces different constraints than an avatar with sight.

A child born in a 'third-world' country faces much different constraints than a child born in a 'first-world' country.

These constraints serve to challenge us within our *physical-matter virtual reality*.

We are all players within the *physical-matter reality* game, with the vast majority of players unaware that they are characters in the game.

Mainstream science clings to the notion that consciousness is found within our physical brains, created by our physical selves, though that is not the case within virtual realities.

Some people are able to function normally with only half a brain, demonstrating that consciousness resides outside the physical, and that our physical bodies are virtual-reality avatars hosting consciousness.

A 2016 article on *businessinsider.com* titled *'This man is missing 90% of his brain yet lives a normal, healthy life'* demonstrates that the brain is a product of consciousness, and not the other way around:

*Not only did his case study cause scientists to question what it takes to survive, **it also challenges our understanding of consciousness.***

In the past, researchers have suggested that consciousness might be linked to various specific brain regions - such as the claustrum, a thin sheet of neurons running between major brain regions, or the visual cortex.

But *if those hypotheses were correct*, then the French man shouldn't be conscious, with the majority of his brain missing.

"<u>Any theory of consciousness</u> has to be able to explain why a person like that, <u>who's missing 90 percent of his neurons</u>, still exhibits normal behaviour," Axel Cleeremans, a cognitive psychologist from the Université Libre de Bruxelles in Belgium, told Quartz.

Self

Google's definition of *"self"* is *"a person's essential being that distinguishes them from others, especially considered as the object of introspection or reflexive action."*

Our consciousness is hosted by an avatar, which is where we derive self. Each avatar in this simulation is unique, and often things beyond our control determine how we perceive ourselves.

The story of our **self** - our gender, race, social status, etc. - **often defines us**, placing constraints on our consciousness which are often difficult to overcome.

Beliefs

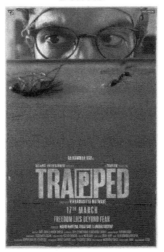

"We often find that <u>we cannot easily give up the tendency to hold</u> <u>rigidly to patterns of thought built up over a long time.</u> We are then caught up in what may be called absolute necessity. This kind of thought leaves no room at all intellectually for any other possibility, while emotionally and physically, it means we take a stance in our feelings, in our bodies, and indeed, in our whole culture, of holding back or resisting. <u>*This stance implies that under no circumstances*</u> <u>*whatsoever can we allow ourselves to give up certain things or change*</u> <u>*them.*</u>" – Physicist David Bohm (1917-1992)

Through time, we acquire beliefs, causing us to get caught in '*belief traps*'. Instead of objectively processing information, we often evaluate information through our *belief-filter.*

This *belief-filter* houses our '*confirmation bias*', often causing us to believe things to be a certain way because **that's how we think they should be**.

A *psychologytoday.com* article titled '*What Is Confirmation Bias?*'

outlines the concept:

Confirmation bias occurs from the direct influence of desire on beliefs. When people would like a certain idea/concept to be true, they end up believing it to be true. They are motivated by wishful thinking. This error leads the individual to **stop gathering information** **when the evidence gathered so far confirms the views (prejudices) one would like to be true.**

Once we have formed a view, **we embrace information that confirms that view while ignoring, or rejecting, information that casts doubt on it.** *Confirmation bias suggests that we don't perceive circumstances objectively. We pick out those bits of data that make us feel good because they confirm our prejudices. Thus,* **we may become prisoners of our assumptions.**

Confirmation bias impacts **all** aspects of our lives. Not confined to religion or politics, *confirmation bias* also plagues the scientific community, causing it to ignore anything that doesn't comply with an '*objective*' physical worldview.

"Fundamental assumptions in general and scientific assumptions in particular are so **hard to overturn because they are based on belief. Beliefs are so hard to overcome because they are irrational and therefore do not yield to logical argument."** - Thomas Campbell

Ego

*"If you identify with a mental position, then if you are wrong, **your mind-based sense of self is seriously threatened with annihilation.** So you as the ego cannot afford to be wrong. <u>To be wrong is to die.</u> Wars have been fought over this, and countless relationships have broken down."* — Eckhart Tolle (author of *'The Power of Now: A Guide to Spiritual Enlightenment'*)

We are slaves to our ego. When our *virtual* story, or reality-paradigm, is threatened, we will lie to others, *and even to ourselves*, to preserve it.

Operating alongside the ego, *the intellect* makes decisions, ensuring that our virtual-reality story persists as we *believe* it should.

Tom Campbell, in *'My Big TOE: Awakening'*, demonstrates that ego impacts everyone, not just *'ego-maniacs'*:

*Ego does not necessarily imply arrogant self - centeredness . Ego comes in an infinite array of expressions — arrogance is only one . **Being timid , unsure , or a worrier are also manifestations of ego . Insecurity and anxiety about that insecurity are common** . How each personality expresses that insecurity and anxiety reflects individual quality and style . The strategies that are used to deal with fear , though common at the top level , are uniquely applied to each individual . **<u>Great ego reflects great fear</u>** ; it does not necessarily reflect great arrogance or great pride , though it may reflect both . Self - centered , self - focused , and self - absorbed are three of the many possible aspects of ego — each of these three can be directed either inwardly (producing timidity) or outwardly (producing arrogance) to **create personality traits that appear to be opposite .***

As our ego grows, our *'quality of consciousness'* declines.

Cultural historian Christopher Lasch coined the term '*pathological narcissism*' to describe the state of post-World War 2 America, though the phrase can generally be used to describe **all** '*advanced*' countries.

In his **1979** book '*The Culture of Narcissism: American Life in an Age of Diminishing Expectations*', Lasch describes the pathological state of humanity:

Our growing dependence on technologies no one seems to understand or control has given rise to feelings of powerlessness and victimization. We find it more and more difficult to achieve a sense of continuity, permanence, or connection with the world around us. Relationships with others are notably fragile; goods are made to be used up and discarded; reality is experienced as an unstable environment of flickering images. Everything conspires to encourage escapist solutions to the psychological problems of dependence, separation, and individuation, and to **discourage the moral realism that makes it possible for human beings to come to terms with** <u>**existential constraints on their power and freedom.**</u>

Our *collective delusion* is fueled by our ego, causing us to cling to an imagined reality-paradigm.

Lasch continues to outline the false premises we collectively perpetuate (also from '*The Culture of Narcissism: American Life in an Age of Diminishing Expectations*'):

The contemporary climate is therapeutic, not religious. People today hunger not for personal salvation, let alone for the restoration of an earlier golden age, but for the feeling, **the momentary illusion, of** <u>**personal well-being, health, and psychic security.**</u>

Materialism has prevailed, and ego-achievements are paramount in this phase of the simulation.

Sigmund Freud (1856-1939), noted founder of '*psychoanalysis*', described the *false-reality-paradigm* inflicting humanity:

*It is impossible to escape the impression that **people commonly use false standards of measurement** — that they seek power, success and wealth for themselves and admire them in others, and that they **underestimate what is of true value in life**.*

This *false-reality-paradigm* manifests as '*mental disorders*' in our virtual-reality society.

A 2011 article on *theatlantic.com* titled '*Why More Americans Suffer From Mental Disorders Than Anyone Else*' describes '*the diagnosed*':

*Over a 12-month period, 27 percent of adults in the U.S. will experience some sort of mental health disorder, making the U.S. the country with the highest prevalence. Mental health disorders include **mood disorders, anxiety disorders, attention deficit/hyperactivity disorder, and substance abuse**. Over one's entire lifetime, the average American has a 47.4 percent chance of having any kind of mental health disorder. **Yes, that's almost one in two.** The projected lifetime prevalence is even higher: for people who reach age 75 it is 55 percent. The WHO data does not take into account eating disorders, personality disorders, and schizophrenia; the incidence of these disorders together is about 15 percent in the U.S., according to the National Institute of Mental Health.*

While the United States is leading the charge, the entire *civilized* world faces essentially the same mental-health scenario (the article continues):

The incidence of mental health disorders varies widely across the globe, and determining the patterns is tricky. After the U.S., Ukraine, Colombia, New Zealand, Lebanon, and France have the next highest rates of mental health disorders of any kind, all falling between 18.9 percent and 21.4 percent in a 12-month period. Japan, the People's Republic of China, Nigeria, and Israel have the lowest rates (between 6.0 percent and 7.4 percent), especially for depression. For substance abuse, the U.S.

is up there, but not the highest: We are topped by South Africa and Ukraine. As with the U.S., when you look at lifetime prevalence in any country, the risk for any disorder goes way up.

The incidence of diagnosed mental health disorders likely pales in comparison to *the 'undiagnosed majority'.*

Aldous Huxley, author of the 1932 dystopian classic *'Brave New World'*, describes the mental disorders afflicting *the undiagnosed majority* (in his 1958 follow-up *'Brave New World Revisited'*):

 The real hopeless victims of mental illness are to be found among those who appear to be most normal. *Many of them are normal because they are so well adjusted to our mode of existence, because their* **human voice has been silenced so early in their lives** *that they do not even struggle or suffer or develop symptoms as the neurotic does. They are normal not in what may be called the absolute sense of the word;* **they are normal only in relation to a profoundly abnormal society. Their perfect adjustment to that abnormal society is a measure of their mental sickness.** *These millions of abnormally normal people, living without fuss in a society to which, if they were fully human beings,* **they ought not to be adjusted.**

In his 1954 book *'The Doors of Perception and Heaven and Hell'*, Huxley outlines how our ego and intellect control us, whether we realize it or not:

All that the conscious ego can do is to formulate wishes, which are then carried out by forces which it controls very little and understands not at all. When it does anything more - when it tries too hard, for example, when it worries, when it becomes apprehensive about the future - it lowers the effectiveness of those forces and may even cause the devitalized body to fall ill. In my present state, awareness was not referred to as ego; it was, so to speak, on its own.

Physicist David Bohm (1917-1992) describes how the act of shedding our deeply-held beliefs is not a 'new age' philosophy, but rather an approach that could constitute a *"revolution in culture"*:

Suppose we were able to share meanings freely without a compulsive urge to impose our view or conform to those of others and without distortion and self-deception. Would this not constitute a ***real revolution in culture.***

Fear

*"Of course, one of the main legitimate functions of thought has always been to help provide security, guaranteeing shelter and food for instance. However, this function went wrong **when the principal source of insecurity came to be the operation of thought itself.**"* – Physicist David Bohm (1917-1992)

In his 1933 inaugural address, former US President Franklin D. Roosevelt proclaimed that *"the only thing we have to fear is...fear itself — nameless, unreasoning, unjustified terror which paralyzes needed efforts to convert retreat into advance."*

Intellectually, we understand that fear is the enemy, but that doesn't prevent fear from subconsciously consuming us.

A *psychologytoday.com* article titled *'The (Only) 5 Fears We All Share'* describes the prevalence of fear:

*A simple and useful definition of **fear** is: An anxious feeling, **caused by our anticipation of some imagined event or experience**.*

*Medical experts tell us that the anxious feeling we get when we're afraid is a standardized biological reaction. **It's pretty much the same set of*** *body signals, whether we're afraid of getting bitten by a dog, getting turned down for a date, or getting our taxes audited.*

*Fear, like all other emotions, is basically **information**. It offers us knowledge and understanding—if we choose to accept it—of our psychobiological status.*

The article places *"ego death"* as our most pervasive fear, keeping us in a constant defensive state of flux:

*That strange idea of "fearing our fears" becomes less strange when we realize that **many of our avoidance reactions**—turning down an invitation to a party if we tend to be uncomfortable in groups; putting off a doctor's appointment; or not asking for a raise—are **instant reflexes that are reactions to the memories of fear.** They happen so quickly that we don't actually experience the full effect of the fear. We experience a "**micro-fear**"—a reaction that's a kind of **shorthand code for the real fear**. **This reflex reaction has the same effect of causing us to evade and avoid as the real fear**. **This is why it's fairly accurate to say that many of our so-called fear reactions are actually the fears of fears.***

These *"micro-fears"* aren't just nagging fears; they often consume us, playing a major role in our lives.

A 2011 *National Institute of Health* (*nih.gov*) article titled *'The consequences of fear'* describes how these fears are largely *figments of our imagination*:

*The cartoon character Charlie Brown once said "I've developed a new philosophy... I only dread one day at a time." If only this were true for many of us in the real world. From transgenic food to industrial chemicals, from radiation to mobile phone towers, the new technologies of our modern world have offered us wonderful new benefits, which also pose a host of new risks. Some of these risks are physically real. **Many are only phantoms of our perceptions**. **Both contribute to an undeniably real sense of worry and apprehension that extends far*** *beyond the next 24 hours.*

*Toxicologists, epidemiologists and risk experts study the physical perils one hazard at a time. But the **cumulative load of modern threats may be creating an even greater risk that is largely overlooked: the risk that arises from <u>misperceiving risks as higher or lower than they actually are</u>. As a result of some of the decisions we make when we are fearful, some of the choices we make when we are not fearful enough, and because of the ways our bodies react to chronically elevated levels of stress, <u>the hazards of risk misperception may be more significant than any of the individual risks about which we fret</u>**. So those who study risk in the name of promoting public health would do well to accept that our perceptions, irrational as they may seem, are real, although we live in a far safer world than just a few generations ago and many of the risks people worry about are small or non-existent. A more comprehensive risk analysis approach must recognize that these **fears pose an actual danger that needs to be understood, accounted for in the analysis, and reduced every bit as much as the threat from any physical hazard.***

Predictably, when we are in a near-constant state of fear, life often feels more like an overwhelming burden than an opportunity for growth and enjoyment.

Much of our fears are rooted in the past; often stemming from childhood. If left unchecked, these childhood fears persist and morph into an all-encompassing *lifestyle.*

An *npr.org* article titled '*What Do Asthma, Heart Disease And Cancer Have In Common? Maybe Childhood Trauma*' describes the prevalence and everlasting damage caused by certain *common* childhood occurrences, which we are often unable to let go:

Two-thirds of Americans are exposed to extreme stress in childhood, *things like divorce, a death in the family or a caregiver's substance* abuse. And this early adversity, if experienced in high enough doses, **"literally gets under our skin, <u>changing people in ways that can endure in their bodies for decades</u>,"** Burke Harris writes in her new book, The Deepest Well: Healing the Long-Term Effects of Childhood Adversity:

"**It can tip a child's developmental trajectory and affect physiology.** It can trigger <u>**chronic inflammation and hormonal changes that can last a lifetime. It can alter the way DNA is read and how cells replicate, and it can dramatically increase the risk for heart disease, stroke, cancer, diabetes — even Alzheimer's**</u>."

Fear often controls us, **because we *choose* to let it**…

Choices

*"Between stimulus and response there is a space. **In that space is <u>our power to choose our response</u>. <u>In our response</u> lies our growth and our freedom."*** *-* Victor E. Frankl (Auschwitz concentration camp survivor; author of '*Man's Search for Meaning*')

Anything with a *'decision space'*, or range of potential decisions requiring free will decision-making, is a player within the **game**.

For many of us, reality often feels like a maze, or *'labyrinth'*, which Google dictionary defines as *"a complicated irregular network of passages or paths in which it is difficult to find one's way."*

Meaningful and immediate feedback is featured in this *physical-matter virtual reality labyrinth*. To ensure opportunities for growth, game players consistently must make decisions with consequences.

We – the consciousness inside the virtual avatars –are constantly faced with choices. The decisions we make aren't always optimal for growth, but the choice is always ours.

Virtual circumstances happen, and outcomes are often sub-optimal, but only we can decide how we react to the *virtual* information, which is arguably more important than the contents of the information itself.

The quality of our decisions determines the *'quality of our consciousness'*.

In this subjective *physical-matter virtual reality*, the game is different for each player. Each player has a different perspective, and faces unique circumstances, processing information through their own unique *data filter*.

Our virtual *'decision space'*, or range of potential decisions, is determined by our physical and emotional makeup.

Physiological and sociological factors play a major role in our *'decision space'*, and the bigger our *decision space*, the more options – or range of choices – we have.

If an avatar has a negative approach and views information through a *negativity-filter*, their *'decision space'* is smaller than that of an optimistic avatar, open to new information and opportunities.

The larger the *decision space*, the more potential for growth.

The Objective

*"After we grow up enough, we no longer need pain to get our attention -- we learn to continue growing while remaining happy and positive because we understand the nature of existence -- we already know what really matters and why. **Our capacity to love and to give** expands without being prodded by pain and misfortune."* - Thomas Campbell

Thomas Campbell's *Big Theory of Everything* posits that *'the larger consciousness system'* has created this *physical-matter reality* as an *'entropy reduction training system'*. We, the players, have been enrolled as a means to reduce the entropy, or disorder, within the *'system'*, to ensure its continued survival.

Campbell also posits that low entropy is expressed as **unconditional love,** defining love as: *"the fundamental expression of low entropy consciousness."*

Unconditional love is a foreign concept to many of us, as society teaches us to 'love ourselves' and put our own needs first.

Much of what we consider love hinges on receiving something in return for our 'love', which stems from fear - **which is the opposite of love.**

*"**When we love, we always strive to become better than we are**. When we strive to become better than we are, **everything around us becomes better too**."* — Paulo Coelho, '*The Alchemist*'

Viktor E. Frankl survived the Auschwitz concentration camp while losing his wife and parents, yet lived the remainder of his life in relative happiness. In his book '*Man's Search for Meaning*', Frankl describes how intense hardships provided the impetus for his growth:

We stumbled on in the darkness, over big stones and through large puddles, along the one road leading from the camp. The accompanying guards kept shouting at us and driving us with the butts of their rifles. Anyone with very sore feet supported himself on his neighbor's arm. Hardly a word was spoken; the icy wind did not encourage talk. Hiding his mouth behind his upturned collar, the man marching next to me whispered suddenly: "If our wives could see us now! I do hope they are better off in their camps and don't know what is happening to us."

*That brought thoughts of my own wife to mind. And as we stumbled on for miles, slipping on icy spots, supporting each other time and again, dragging one another up and onward, nothing was said, but we both knew: each of us was thinking of his wife. Occasionally I looked at the sky, where the stars were fading and the pink light of the morning was beginning to spread behind a dark bank of clouds. But my mind clung to my wife's image, imagining it with an uncanny acuteness. **I heard her answering me, saw her smile, her frank and encouraging look**. **Real or not**, her look was then more luminous than the sun which was beginning to rise.*

124

*A thought transfixed me: for the first time in my life I saw the truth as it is set into song by so many poets, proclaimed as the final wisdom by so many thinkers. **The truth—that love is the ultimate and the highest goal to which man can aspire.** Then I grasped the meaning of the greatest secret that human poetry and human thought and belief have to impart: **The salvation of man is through love and in love.** I understood how a man who has nothing left in this world still may know bliss, be it only for a brief moment, in the contemplation of his beloved. In a position of utter desolation, when man cannot express himself in positive action, when his only achievement may consist in enduring his sufferings in the right way—an honorable way—in such a position man can, through loving contemplation of the image he carries of his beloved, achieve fulfillment. For the first time in my life I was able to understand the meaning of the words, "The angels are lost in perpetual contemplation of an infinite glory...."*[6]

The concept of unconditional love does not imply passivity in the prospect of danger, or naïveté in one's approach. With the world population seemingly caught in the *'prisoner's dilemma'*, moving from a fear-based society to a love-based society is our *virtual* objective.

*"Every great and deep difficulty bears in itself its own solution. **It forces us to change our thinking in order to find it**."* - Physicist Max Planck (1858-1947)

In our current *fear-based* virtual-reality society, large-scale **forced** changes often add to fear and despair.

Dystopian author George Orwell - author of *'1984'* and *'Animal Farm'* - exposes how *fear-based* societies *de-evolve*. In *'Animal Farm'*, Orwell demonstrates how leadership in *fear-based* societies does not benefit the group as a whole, infamously explaining that: *"All animals are created equal, **but some are more equal than others**."*

125

In fear-based societies, those in positions of power place self-preservation over the welfare of the group.

In '*Animal Farm*', Comrade Napoleon describes why the pigs – the decision makers – require certain privileges not available to the *general population*:

*Comrades!' he cried. 'You do not imagine, I hope, that we pigs are doing this in a spirit of selfishness and privilege? Many of us actually dislike milk and apples. I dislike them myself. Our sole object in taking these things is to preserve our health. Milk and apples (**this has been proved by Science, comrades**) contain substances absolutely necessary to the well-being of a pig. We pigs are brainworkers. The whole management and organisation of this farm depend on us. **Day and night we are watching over your welfare**. It is for your sake that we drink the milk and eat those apples.*

The *unconditional love* that Thomas Campbell describes is only possible through *ego-reduction*, and improving ourselves individually at the '*being level*'.

The '*being level*', as Campbell describes, is the state which we truly are, not the state that we think we are, or the façade we present to the world.

The '*being level*' is the true measure of our '*quality of consciousness*'.

If we see a proverbial 'little old lady crossing the street', the action we take often factors in who is watching and how we will be perceived by others. Most will help her across the street for ego-driven purposes, and because we **know** it's the right thing to do.

Our '*being level*' determines whether we help the 'little old lady' cross the street because we truly care for her well-being, or because our ego and intellect tell us we should.

Tom Campbell, in *'My Big TOE: Awakening'*, outlines the process:

*Improving the quality of your consciousness, energizing spiritual growth, and gaining a Big Picture perspective are **not accomplished by changing what you do, but by <u>changing what you are</u>**.*

Self-Destruction

Improved '*quality of consciousness*' is not attained through governmental mandates or increased intellectual understanding, but instead occurs through *individual* change.

The physical body provides a model to which humanity may aspire.

Within our physical avatar, cells work together holistically to benefit the whole. Cells within the brain don't protest because they are working harder than the cells within the hand; our heart does not decide to shut down because our little toe isn't pulling its weight.

This process is also found in nature, as '*superorganisms*' work together to achieve impressive results.

Ant colonies are considered '*superorganisms*', inspiring the study of '*ant colony optimization*'. A book titled '*Ant Colony Optimization*', as described on *mit.org*, demonstrates how ant-colonies also provide a working model which humanity can aspire:

The complex social behaviors of ants have been much studied by science, *and* ***computer scientists are now finding that these behavior patterns*** *can provide models for solving difficult combinatorial optimization problems*. The attempt to develop algorithms inspired by one aspect of ant behavior, the ability to find what computer scientists would call shortest paths, has become the field of ant colony optimization (ACO), the most successful and widely recognized algorithmic technique based on ant behavior.

'*Superorganisms*' don't function as hollow dictatorships, but instead allow for maximum **individual growth** within a cohesive group dynamic.

An *Arizona State University* article (*ASU.edu*) titled '*Secrets of a Superorganism*' demonstrates this phenomenon:

*An ant colony is like a factory. Nestmates work together to convert resources (food) into products (more ants). This process is made more efficient through division of labor, where different individuals specialize on different jobs. The queen has the very specific role of laying eggs, which she spends most of her life doing. Worker ants perform other duties, often depending on their age. Younger ants work inside the nest, taking care of the queen and her brood. **Older workers go outside to gather food and defend the nest against enemies. Despite her size and royal title, the queen doesn't boss the workers around. Instead, <u>workers decide which tasks to perform based on personal preferences, interactions with nestmates, and cues from the environment.</u>***

Salmon also display selfless attributes, selflessly working to perpetuate their survival.

An *inc.com* article titled '*1 Surprising Lesson About Failure You Can Learn From Salmon (Yes, the Fish)*' explains:

In the winter, a female salmon finds a gravel bed in clear water to lay up to 5,000 eggs. Of those thousands of eggs, some aren't fertilized, a few get washed away, while others are covered in dirt erosion.

Still, most of the eggs hatch into alevins and start off in a small stream.

Some are eaten or die of weakness before. After about a year, the salmon move downstream for more food and space before traveling to sea.

*The fish then make the big trek to the ocean. Along the way, **hundreds are fished up, eaten by bigger fish, or die from sickness and pollution**. The ones that survive remain in the ocean until they become healthy and strong adults.*

After awhile, the salmon fight against the currents to return to the tiny stream where they were born. A number of them die of exhaustion along the way. Out of the thousands of eggs in the stream, less than a hundred salmon make it back to their place of birth to continue the cycle of life.

***The chances of an egg growing into an adult salmon are less than 1 percent**. But the more eggs a salmon lays, **the higher the probability** that its children will live long enough to return to its birthplace.*

'Superorganisms' don't dwell in the past or fear the future. **They live in the present.**

Living in the present is a foreign concept to most of us, as we incessantly distract ourselves from what is occurring around us at any given moment.

Breaking free from a life of preoccupation can be difficult.

Sometimes hitting *'rock bottom'* can cause us to re-examine our lives. Eckert Tolle, author of *'The Power of Now'*, describes the catalyst for his life-change (as quoted in an article on *theage.com* titled *'Why Now is Bliss)':*

*I couldn't live with myself any longer. And in this a question arose without an answer: who is the 'I' that cannot live with the self? What is the self? I felt drawn into a void! I didn't know at the time that what really happened was **the mind-made self, with its heaviness, its problems, that lives between the unsatisfying past and the fearful future, collapsed. It dissolved**. The next morning I woke up and* *everything was so peaceful.* **The peace was there because there was no self. Just a sense of presence or "beingness," just observing and watching.**

The Secret

*"We do whatever comes to us at the moment -- **what we do matters little -- the intent behind the doing is an expression of our being that matters much. The feedback from the doing informs the quality of the being to modify its intent** -- this is the bootstrap by which we pull ourselves up."* - Physicist Tom Campbell

'The Secret', the *'law of attraction'*, and *'the power of positive thinking'* are not mysterious new-age enigmas, but instead fundamental characteristics within our *physical-matter reality* simulation.

Isaac Newton's third law of motion *believes* that every action has an equal and opposite reaction; that everything that happens in our *presumed physical-matter reality* is a result of cause and effect.

In a virtual-reality system seeking to lower its entropy, the physical is secondary to a much greater *force*: **Intent**.

"Intent modifies future probability." –Tom Campbell

132

A 1993 social experiment in Washington, D.C., demonstrates the power of intent.

Published by the *Institute of Science, Technology, and Public Policy* (*istpp.org*), the study *'Effects of Group Practice of the Transcendental Meditation Program on Preventing Violent Crime in Washington, DC: Results of the National Demonstration Project, June-July 1993'* provides a model in which intent modifies future probability on a meta-scale:

*This study presents the final results of a two-month prospective experiment to reduce violent crime in Washington, DC. On the basis of previous research **it was hypothesized that the level of violent crime in the District of Columbia would drop significantly** with the creation of a large group of participants in the Transcendental Meditation® and TM-Sidhi® programs to **increase coherence and reduce stress** in the District.*

This National Demonstration Project to Reduce Violent Crime and Improve Governmental Effectiveness brought approximately 4,000 participants in the Transcendental Meditation and TM-Sidhi programs to the United States national capital from June 7 to July 30, 1993. A 27-member independent Project Review Board consisting of sociologists and criminologists from leading universities, representatives from the police department and government of the District of Columbia, and civic leaders approved in advance the research protocol for the project and monitored its progress.

*The dependent variable in the research was **weekly violent crime**, as measured by the Uniform Crime Report program of the Federal Bureau of Investigation; violent crimes include homicide, rape, aggravated assault, and robbery. This data was obtained from the District of Columbia Metropolitan Police Department for 1993 as well as for the preceding five years (1988-1992). Additional data used for control purposes included weather variables (temperature, precipitation, humidity), daylight hours, changes in police and community anti-crime activities, prior crime trends in the District of Columbia, and concurrent crime trends in neighboring cities. Average weekly temperature was*

*significantly correlated with homicides, rapes and assaults (HRA crimes),
as has also been found in previous research; therefore temperature was
used as a control variable in the main analysis of HRA crimes. Using time
series analysis, violent crimes were analyzed separately in terms of **HRA
crimes (crimes against the person)** and robbery (monetary crimes), as
well as together.*

The results of the study leave no doubt that **intent is the main
determinant** within our *physical-matter reality* simulation:

*Based on the results of the study, the steady state gain (long-term
effect) associated with a permanent group of 4,000 participants in the
Transcendental Meditation and TM-Sidhi programs was **calculated as <u>a
48% reduction in HRA crimes in the District of Columbia.</u>***

***Given the strength of these results, their consistency with the positive
results of previous research, the grave human and financial costs of
violent crime, and the lack of other effective and scientific methods to
reduce crime, policy makers are urged to <u>apply this approach on a
large scale for the benefit of society.</u>***

The Placebo Effect

The *placebo effect* demonstrates that our intent plays a key role in our lives, simultaneously serving as a major thorn in the side of the pharmaceutical industry.

A 2009 article on *wired.com* titled *'Placebos Are Getting More Effective. Drugmakers Are Desperate to Know Why'* demonstrates this *bizarre* phenomenon:

Despite historic levels of industry investment in R&D, the US Food and Drug Administration approved only 19 first-of-their-kind remedies in 2007—the fewest since 1983—and just 24 in 2008. ***Half of all drugs that fail in late-stage trials drop out of the pipeline due to their inability to beat sugar pills.***

The *placebo effect* often prevents new pharmaceuticals from reaching the market, also casting doubt on the legitimacy of *established* drugs (the article continues):

Some products that have been on the market for decades, like Prozac, are **faltering in more recent follow-up tests**. In many cases, these are the compounds that, in the late '90s, made Big Pharma more profitable than Big Oil. But if these same drugs were vetted now, **the FDA might not approve some of them. Two comprehensive analyses of antidepressant trials have uncovered a dramatic increase in placebo response since the 1980s. One estimated that the so-called effect size (a measure of statistical significance) in placebo groups had nearly doubled over that time.**

It's not that the old meds are getting weaker, drug developers say. It's as if the placebo effect is somehow getting stronger.

In our *physical-matter virtual reality*, **our thoughts, forming our intent, influence future outcomes**.

A 2015 article on *harvard.edu* titled '*The placebo effect: Amazing and real'* describes how the non-physical, or **consciousness**, influences the physical:

*Recent research on the placebo effect only confirms **how powerful it can be** — and that the benefits of a placebo treatment **aren't just "all in your head." Measureable physiological changes can be observed in those taking a placebo, similar to those observed among people taking effective medications. In <u>particular, blood pressure, heart rate, and blood test results have been shown to improve among subsets of research subjects who responded to a placebo.</u>***

When we *believe* that our physical symptoms will improve, they often improve. **When we believe that they won't, they often don't.**

The *placebo effect* also demonstrates how persistent fear, apprehension, and negativity produce equally negative outcomes (the article continues):

Nocebo: Placebo's evil twin

*The power of suggestion is a double-edged sword. If you expect a treatment to help you, it's more likely to do so. **And if you expect a treatment will be harmful, you are more likely to experience negative effects.** That phenomenon is called the "nocebo effect" (from the Latin "I shall harm"). **For example, if you tell a person that a headache is a common side effect of a particular medication, that person is more likely to report headaches even if they are actually taking a placebo.** <u>The power of expectation</u> (Stith: intent) **is formidable and probably plays a significant role in the benefits** and **the side effects of commonly prescribed medications.***

The *nocebo effect* has a firm grip on much of humanity, evidenced by our poor collective health. The *world healthcare crisis* would seem to be less a result of solely physical processes, largely stemming from our fears and apprehensions.

A 2011 article on *heartmath.org* titled '*You Can Change Your DNA*' outlines the cause and effect of the persistent underlying fear subconsciously controlling our thoughts and actions:

Stem cell biologist and bestselling author Bruce Lipton, Ph.D., says the distinction between genetic determinism and epigenetics is important.

*"The difference between these two is significant because **this fundamental belief called genetic determinism literally means that our lives, which are defined as our physical, physiological and emotional behavioral traits, are controlled by the genetic code,"** Lipton said in an interview with the online magazine, Superconsciousness. "**This kind of belief system provides a visual picture of people being victims: If the genes control our life function, then our lives are being controlled by things outside of our ability to change them. This leads to victimization that the illnesses and diseases that run in families are propagated through the passing of genes associated with those attributes. Laboratory evidence shows this is not true."***

A Steady Diet of Quantum Nutrients

*"When we have negative emotions such as **anger, anxiety and dislike or hate, or think negative thoughts such as 'I hate my job,' 'I don't like so and so' or 'Who does he think he is?', we experience stress and our energy reserves are redirected**," an article on HMI's website explains. **This causes a portion of our energy reserves, which otherwise would be put to work maintaining, repairing and regenerating our complex biological systems, <u>to instead confront the stresses these negative thoughts and feelings create.</u>***

"Negative thoughts and feelings" manifest as physical maladies, causing a significant decrease in our quality of life, as well as our *'quality of consciousness'*.

A 2017 article on *independent.co.uk* titled *'Broken heart can cause same type of long-lasting damage as a heart attack'* describes how our thoughts profoundly influence not just our emotional state, but also our physical well-being:

***<u>Severe emotional stress can prompt a sudden heart condition that poses the same sort of long-term damage as a heart attack</u>**, new research has found.*

Takotsubo cardiomyopathy – or "broken heart syndrome" - affects at least 3,000 people in the UK and is typically triggered by traumatic life events such as bereavement.

*During an attack, the **heart muscle weakens to the point where it can no longer function as effectively.***

*While previous research had suggested that the damage caused was temporary, scientists at the University of Aberdeen have now found that **<u>the effects can be permanent, like a heart attack.</u>***

Operation Entropy-Reduction

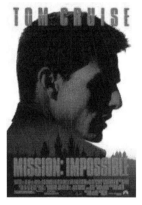

*"**<u>Courage and determination</u>** will grow sufficiently to overcome fear if the intent to succeed is sufficiently strong , steady , and clear."* - Tom Campbell; *'My Big TOE: Awakening'*

In our fast-paced, chaotic lives, slowing down long enough to catch our breath, let alone to *'lower our entropy'*, may seem like a pipe-dream.

Science clearly demonstrates that we are happier when we are in-the-moment, and not distracted by lingering fear and apprehension.

A 2010 *scientificamerican.com* article titled *'A Wandering Mind is an Unhappy One'* outlines the research:

*In a recent study published in Science, Killingsworth and Gilbert discovered that an unnervingly **large fraction of our thoughts - almost half - are not related to what we're doing.** Surprisingly, **we tended to be elsewhere even for casual and presumably enjoyable activities, like watching TV or having a conversation. While you might hope all this mental wandering is taking us to happier places, the data say otherwise**. Just like the wise traditions teach, **<u>we're happiest when</u>***

139

thought and action are aligned, even if they're only aligned to wash dishes.

Letting go of fear and ego, or disengaging from their *data streams*, allows us to experience the present moment without apprehension and irrational worry (the article continues):

*In addition to awakening us to just how much our minds wander, **the study clearly showed that we're happiest when thinking about what we're doing.** Although imagining pleasant alternatives was naturally preferable to imagining unpleasant ones, **the happiest scenario was to not be imagining at all.** A person who is ironing a shirt and thinking about ironing is happier than a person who is ironing and thinking about a sunny getaway.*

*What about the kinds of activities we do, though? Surely, the hard-partiers and world travelers among us are happier than the quiet ones who stay at home and tuck in early? **Not necessarily.** According to the data from the Harvard group's study, **the particular way you spend your day doesn't tell much about how happy you are. Mental presence - the matching of thought to action - is a much better predictor of happiness.***

The happy upshot of this study is that it suggests a wonderfully simple prescription for greater happiness: think about what you're doing.

A 2010 *ucla.edu* article titled *'Mind over matter: Study shows we consciously exert control over individual neurons'* demonstrates that **we have the ability** to control our thoughts:

*Now a collaboration between UCLA scientists and colleagues from the California Institute of Technology has shown that humans can actually regulate the activity of specific neurons in the brain, increasing the firing rate of some while decreasing the rate of others. And study subjects were able to do so by **manipulating an image on a computer screen using only their thoughts.***

Reporting in the Oct. 28 issue of the journal Nature, UCLA professor of

neurosurgery Itzhak Fried and Caltech neuroscientist Christof Koch,
along with colleagues, recorded the activity of single neurons in patients
implanted with intracranial electrodes (for clinical reasons) and
demonstrated that humans regulate the activity of their neurons to
intentionally alter the outcome of all this stimulation.

Our thoughts and biases towards negativity are not easily changed,
requiring a similar approach to the first two laws of *Alcoholics
Anonymous* (AA).

The first step is acknowledging that we are driven by fear and ego. The
second step is working with a *'higher power'*, in this case *'the larger
consciousness system'*, to improve the state of our being, or our *'quality
of consciousness'*.

*"A quiet mind cureth **all**."* – English author Robert Burton (1577-1640)

'Monkey mind' is a Buddhist term used to describe the incessant internal chatter and endless distractions which often consume our intellect.

The stresses of the day, smart phones, money, jobs, kids, crime, politics, and a myriad of other issues steadily rush in and out of our minds, removing our focus from the present and suspending many of us in a state of *gnawing apprehension*.

The constant bombardment of information often leaves us in a state of flux, and calming our *'monkey mind'* allows us to *process the data* in a more constructive manner.

Unlike a computer, our minds don't have a firewall and virus protection to keep *bad data from infecting our system*, **requiring that we take matters into our own hands.**

Meditation, while often associated with *eastern mysticism* or the *'new-*

age', is more practically viewed as the act of disengaging from the myriad data streams tethering us to our physical-reality story, allowing us to quiet the *'monkey mind'*, eliminate fear and ego, and get in-tune with our *being level*.

French philosopher Voltaire (1694-1778) describes how *meditation* is not about acquiring more beliefs, but instead disengaging from our deeply held ones:

<u>Meditation is the dissolution of thoughts</u> *in eternal awareness or pure consciousness* **without objectification**, *knowing* **without thinking**, *merging finitude in infinity.*

Tom Campbell, in *'My Big TOE: Awakening'*, de-mystifies *meditation*:

There are many effective paths to personal growth – meditation is only one . Within the wide range of practices that circumscribe what we have loosely defined as meditation , there are many different types , approaches , and methods . Because it is the easiest , most effective , and universally applicable , ***a simple mental - awareness meditation is the path of choice for most teachers and students who have no dogma to propagate .*** *Within this subset of meditation , there are many differing techniques . The technique you choose is not as important as* ***<u>the application of steady effort</u>*** *– so choose a technique that suits you . Within this genre of meditation ,* ***<u>you do not actually have to learn how to meditate ; you need only to learn how to stop blocking the meditation state from occurring naturally .</u>***

A 2017 *businessinsider.com* article titled *'After interviewing 140 people at the top of their fields, Tim Ferriss realized almost all of them share the same habit'* demonstrates how meditation is not solely a 'new-age' belief, but also a results-oriented lifestyle **choice**:

"Despite the fact that these are people from tennis to surfing to cryptocurrency to fill-in-the-blank, like any field you can possibly imagine

— some type of **morning mindfulness or meditation practice would span I'd say 90% of the respondents."**

There's no denying that "mindfulness" (a type of meditation) is a buzzword and meditation a trend in business right now, but that doesn't mean that you should write them off, Ferriss explained.

"**Meditation has a branding problem**," he said. "A lot of people would think of yoga instructors playing didgeridoos, swinging dream-catchers over their heads — and they wouldn't be entirely wrong in a lot of cases."

But at the heart of it, <u>meditation is a simple practice that is about training the mind's control over its emotions.</u>

"**So meditation, or mindfulness practice, it's really about, to me, <u>decreasing emotional reactivity so you can proactively create your day and create your life</u>; versus, just being a walking reflex that sometimes screws up**," Ferriss said.

Author Dan Harris, in his book '*10% Happier: How I Tamed the Voice in My Head, Reduced Stress Without Losing My Edge, and Found Self-Help That Actually Works*', describes how taming the '*monkey mind*' is the **only path** to achieving lasting happiness:

The route of true happiness, the Buddha argued, was to achieve a visceral understanding of impermanence, which would take you off the emotional roller coaster and allow you to see your dramas and desires through a wider lens. To truly tame the 'monkey mind' and defeat our habitual tendency toward clinging, **meditation was the prescription**, and sitting and actively facing the 'voice in your head' mindfully for **a few minutes a day** might be the hardest thing you'll ever do. **<u>Accept that challenge and improve your life drastically.</u>** It's about mitigation, not alleviation. It's that simple. **<u>The only way out is through.</u>**

Once our '*monkey mind*' is calmed, we are able stop processing information through a '*fear-filter*'.

Untangling our deep-rooted, and often irrational, fears and beliefs **is a process,** and not something that happens overnight.

Tom Campbell, in '*My Big TOE: Awakening*', outlines the elusive nature of our true selves:

*Most of us have deeply held and ingrained ways of thinking and being whether we are intellectually aware of them or not. What is deeply ingrained in us is **nearly impossible for us to notice – it becomes part of the invisible inner core of our being**. It is a fact that subtle belief systems circumscribe our personal reality. It is also a fact that **most of our beliefs lie beyond the easy reach of our intellects**. <u>**Outside our awareness, they literally define, and thus also limit, what we allow ourselves to perceive and interpret as reality.**</u>*

Many of us have been carrying our deep-rooted fears and beliefs with us since childhood.

An article on s*mithsonian.com* titled '*What Happens in the Brain When We Feel Fear*' demonstrates the prevalence and impact of our *deep-seated fears*:

*Abnormal levels of fear and anxiety can lead to significant distress and dysfunction and limit a person's ability for success and joy of life. Nearly one in four people experiences a form of anxiety disorder during their lives, and **nearly 8 percent experience post-traumatic stress disorder (PTSD)**.*

*Disorders of anxiety and fear include phobias, social phobia, generalized anxiety disorder, separation anxiety, PTSD and obsessive compulsive disorder. These conditions usually begin at a young age, and without appropriate treatment can become chronic and debilitating and **affect a person's life trajectory**.*

Like the *butterfly effect*, stressful childhood occurrences, such as being the laughing stock of jokes or being bullied by classmates, often has a profound long-term impact.

In our attempts to ensure that we never experience those feelings again, we erect barriers, facades, and stories, often contributing to lifelong struggles with anger, trust, and companionship.

Bringing our fears out into the open is the first step to realizing that **our fears are often irrational and able to be overcome.**

The traditional psychological approach is to have patients discuss and relive past traumas, often *over and over* again.

Through meditation, however, *identifying and facing* our deep-seated fears is paramount, while dwelling on the past holds little to no value.

Tom Campbell describes this process as '*growing up*', or improving our selves at the '*being level*'; outlining the objective in '*My Big TOE:*

146

Awakening':

*Spiritual growth, improving the quality of your consciousness, is about changing your attitude, expanding your awareness, **outgrowing your fears, reducing your ego, and improving your capacity to love**.*

Cheat Codes

"The journey of a thousand miles begins with a single step." – Lao Tzu (ancient Chinese philosopher)

With patience, persistence, and practice, *entropy reduction* – which translates to a more meaningful and joyful life - is a *real* option **available to all players** within this virtual-reality simulation.

Arriving at a meditative state often seems difficult, but certain *strategies* have proven to be more fruitful than others.

Imagine staring intently into a babbling brook; the contours of the rushing water hold our attention, keeping the *'monkey mind'* actively engaged and allowing our attention to gaze inwards.

Staring into a babbling brook may not be a realistic option for most of us, but there are other more practical strategies which can be used to quiet the *'monkey mind'*.

Some are able to quiet their *'monkey mind'* at will, while others use tactics such as deep breathing or repeating sounds, known as *mantras*.

Tom Campbell de-mystifies *mantras* in *'My Big TOE: Awakening'*:

*Some traditions call this **mental busy - work** assignment a " mantra . " Traditionally this is a sound of some sort , but in this Big TOE we are bound only by science , not tradition . We quickly move to toss belief , dogma , and ritual out of the window and focus , by experimental result , only on the active ingredients of mantra . Science allows the concept of mantra to be generalized to accommodate the various ways we take in and process information through our five senses . Typically , people tend to take in most of their experiential input data through their ears (**auditory**) , eyes (**visual**) or sense of touch (**kinesthetic**) . Many people absorb information more effectively through one of these avenues of* *data input than they do through the others . Over the previous decade or so , the popular literature is full of assessments of personality type and characteristics by data input preference . It makes no sense to force everyone down the traditional auditory path – some people simply do not get it that way .*

Campbell continues to provide *the secret* to an effective mantra:

*For the audio types , we need a sound that means nothing , is two syllables , and ends in a soothing or vibratory sound . Here are a few examples of proven quality – take your pick or make up one of your own : " sehr - ring " , " da - room " , " ra - zing " , " ca - ouhn " , " sah - roon " , and " sher - loom . " For a simple multi - syllable repetitive string (chant) , try : " ah - lum - bar - dee - dum – ah - lum - baa - dee - dum . " When the " bar " and " baa " regularly interchange themselves effortlessly , you will be well on your way . **These are sounds , not words – it is important that they carry no intellectual meaning . The point of this exercise is to quiet your operative intellect so that you can experience consciousness directly by reducing the variations , comparisons , and contrasts that your ego - intellect imposes upon consciousness .** Feel free to mix and match – put any of the first syllables in front of any of the second syllables to produce no fewer than thirty - six unique mantras . For most people , it won't make much difference which sound is used , but if one sound feels more natural than the others , use it . Obsessive - compulsive types should take care not to get wrapped around the axle trying to find the best one – **any will do .***

Another approach, referred to as '*brainwave entrainment*', preoccupies our intellect with **different types of stimuli**, proving to be an effective strategy for calming the '*monkey mind*'.

A 2008 study published *on pubmed.gov* titled '*A comprehensive review of the psychological effects of brainwave entrainment*' researched the potential for "*rhythmic stimuli to alter brainwave frequency*":

*Brainwave entrainment (BWE), which uses rhythmic stimuli to alter brainwave frequency and thus brain states, has been investigated and used since the late 1800s, **yet many clinicians and scientists are***

unaware of its existence. *We aim to raise awareness and discuss its potential by presenting a systematic review of the literature from peer-reviewed journals on the psychological effects of BWE.*

The study draws strong conclusions:

Findings to date suggest that BWE is **an effective therapeutic tool. People suffering from cognitive functioning deficits, stress, pain, headache/migraines, PMS, and behavioral problems benefited from BWE.** *However, more controlled trials are needed to test additional protocols with outcomes.*

'Eye movement desensitization and reprocessing', known as *EMDR*, has shown to be an effective application of *'brainwave entrainment'*.

EMDR 'therapy' incorporates *'bilateral stimulation'*, distracting the intellect with tactile (touch), audible, and/or visual stimuli. The devices typically used to administer *EMDR* have visual (alternating side-by-side lights), tactile (alternating pulsars/buzzers for each hand), and audible (alternating audio) stimuli options, for those seeking **a more powerful and/or multi-faceted approach** to quieting the *'monkey mind'*.

EMDR has been shown to quickly calm the loudest *'monkey mind'*, including those suffering from PTSD.

A 2014 study in the *National Institute of Health* (*nih.gov*) titled *'The Role of Eye Movement Desensitization and Reprocessing (EMDR) Therapy in Medicine: Addressing the Psychological and Physical Symptoms Stemming from Adverse Life Experiences'* demonstrates the efficacy of this approach:

A substantial body of research shows that adverse life experiences contribute to both psychological and biomedical pathology. **Eye movement desensitization and reprocessing (EMDR) therapy is an empirically validated treatment** *for trauma,* **including such negative life experiences as commonly present in medical practice. The positive**

therapeutic outcomes rapidly achieved without homework or detailed
description of the disturbing event **offer the medical community an**
efficient treatment approach with a wide range of applications.

By *quickly* preoccupying our *'monkey mind'* with various *scientifically-proven* stimuli, we are able to quickly attain the meditative state needed to face – and overcome - our fears (the study concludes):

A substantial amount of research indicates that adverse life experiences may be the basis for a wide range of psychological and physiologic symptoms. EMDR therapy research has shown that **processing** **memories of such experiences results in the rapid amelioration of** **negative emotions, beliefs, and physical sensations.** **Reports have** **indicated potential applications for** **patients with stress-related** **disorders,** **as well as those suffering from a wide range of physical** **conditions. The medical community can also benefit from the use of** **EMDR therapy for prevention and rehabilitative services to support** **both patients and family members. A thorough assessment of** **potential experiential contributors can be beneficial. If relevant, EMDR** **therapy can allow medical personnel to quickly determine the degree** **to which distressing experiences are a contributing factor and to** **efficiently address the problem through memory processing that can** **help facilitate both psychological and physical resolution***. Rigorous research of the use of EMDR therapy with patients suffering from the conditions identified in the ACE Study can further contribute to our understanding of the potential for both remediation and preventive care.*

EMDR is clinically referred to as a form of *'psychotherapy'*, and the 'treatment' sessions are typically therapist-led. For those seeking a do-it-yourself approach, *EMDR* (*"bilateral stimulation"*) devices can be purchased online, as the device itself is essentially 'non-scientific'; consisting of alternating flashing lights, alternating pulsars, and alternating audible sounds.

(Stith note: It is of the author's opinion that these devices are
invaluable and should be considered by anyone seeking to reduce -
***and ultimately eliminate* - their *'monkey mind';* of course, be sure to**

consult a trained medical professional prior to trying such device (alternating beeps, buzzes, and lights) at home!!!)

With consistent intent, practice and persistence, Campbell explains, effectively managing our '*monkey mind*' and switching reality frames – or data streams - can be done at-will and without the aid of rituals and devices.

With minimal profit-potential, calming the '*monkey mind*' is ignored by mainstream medicine and science, placing the onus of responsibility on **the individual.**

Focusing Intent

"Ask, and it shall be given you; seek, and ye shall find; knock, and it shall be opened unto you." – King James Bible; *Matthew 7:7*

In *physical-matter reality*, the intellect is invaluable, helping us navigate our physical-matter lives.

In *non-physical-matter reality*, the intellect is merely a hindrance.

As we reduce our fears, we grow more in-tune with *'the larger consciousness system'*, where our *'being level'* resides.

Thomas Campbell refers to this space as *'point consciousness'*; the place where our consciousness exists outside of our *self*.

Aldous Huxley, author of *'Brave New World,'* describes how our ego and intellect have a purpose, but true growth comes from *'point consciousness'* (quoted in *'Moksha: Aldous Huxley's Classic Writings on Psychedelics and the Visionary Experience'):*

*The ordinary waking consciousness is a very useful and, on most occasions, **an indispensable state of mind;** but it is by no means the only form of consciousness, nor in all circumstances the best. Insofar as he **transcends his ordinary self and his ordinary mode of awareness, the mystic is able to enlarge his vision, to look more deeply into the unfathomable miracle of existence.***

*The mystical experience is doubly valuable; it is valuable because it gives the experiencer **a better understanding of himself and the world and because it may help him to lead a less self-centered and more creative life.***

In *'point consciousness'*, we have the choice to simply *'be'*, or we can focus our intent to pursue broader and more meaningful endeavors.

Focusing our intent allows us to heal others, go *'out of body'*, modify future probability, and participate in a wide range of other *learning* applications, according to Campbell.

The previously mentioned study that showed a 48% reduction in serious Washington D.C. crime, titled *'Effects of Group Practice of the Transcendental Meditation Program on Preventing Violent Crime in Washington, DC: Results of the National Demonstration Project, June-July 1993'*, demonstrates that a focused intent can have a profound impact, and hints at the potential for *real and profound* change.

Tom Campbell explains the transition from reducing fear and ego to exploring the bigger picture – and actively focusing intent - in *'My Big TOE: Awakening'*:

*Do you see why meditation is almost **universally prescribed as the first step – the doorway to understanding and exploring consciousness , as well as to the attainment of spiritual growth** ? It makes sense that a*

program to develop your consciousness should naturally start with
finding and becoming acquainted with that consciousness . There are
other methods , but they apply less universally , are more difficult to
learn , and are much more difficult to teach . Meditation will work
wonderfully when you are ready . You may first need to work on getting
ready by developing an honest desire to grow spiritually and the courage
to pursue Big Truth to its conclusion . You may need to first overcome
some of the fear and cultural beliefs to which you have become attached
. How does meditation clear out the clutter and reduce the noise level of
a mind caught in a self - referential endless loop of obfuscating circular
logic ? The technique is simple and straightforward – the trappings of
ritual , dogma , belief , and physical process are mostly irrelevant . You
simply stop the incessant operational , self - referential , contrast
producing chatter of the mind by filling the mind up with something less
distracting , less self - focused and less obsessively driven . While the
mind is preoccupied with non - operative busy - work , you can
experience the still center of your being . Eventually , after much practice
, you can let go of the mental busy - work and **explore the larger reality**
of consciousness from an imperturbable , still , and quiet place that
will **_slowly develop and grow larger at the center of your being ._**

The *"imperturbable , still , and quiet place"* is not a space for only the
select few, but is a place which we all have been, and where we all can
go, if we just get out of our own way.

Bruce Lee, in his book '*Tao of Jeet Kune Do*', describes the power of 'the
system' and how *self-consciousness* holds us back from consciously
interacting with '*the larger consciousness system*', which we are **all** part
of:

I'm moving and not moving at all. I'm like the moon underneath the
waves that ever go on rolling and rocking. It is not, "I am doing this," but
*rather, an inner realization that "**this is happening through me**," or "it is*
doing this for me." **_The consciousness of self is the greatest hindrance_**
to the proper execution of all physical action.

"*For the last four hundred years, an **unstated assumption** of science is that human intention cannot affect **what we call 'physical reality**.' Our experimental research of the past decade shows that, for today's world and under the right conditions, this assumption is no longer correct. **<u>We humans are much more than we think we are</u>** and **Psychoenergetic Science** continues to expand the proof of it.*" – Stanford Professor Emeritus William Tiller

Professor William Tiller has worked in the mainstream his entire career (as posted on *tillerinstitute.com*):

*Fellow to the American Academy for the Advancement of Science, Professor Emeritus William A. Tiller, of Stanford University's Department of **<u>Materials Science</u>**, spent 34 years in academia after 9 years as an advisory physicist with the Westinghouse Research Laboratories.*

He has published over 250 conventional scientific papers, 3 books and several patents. In parallel, for over 30 years, he has been avocationally

pursuing serious experimental and theoretical study of the field of psychoenergetics which will very likely become an integral part of "tomorrow's" physics. In this new area, he has published an additional 100 scientific papers and four seminal books.

Professor Tiller veered from his mainstream peers, concluding that *consciousness* interacts with - **and modifies** – *physical-matter reality.*

In a presentation published on *Tillerinstitute.com* titled *'An Introduction to Psychoenergetic Science & Information Medicine',* Tiller outlines four experiments demonstrating the *mind over matter* phenomenon, and the profound implications:

*All four target experiments were robustly successful, proving that, in today's world, the unstated assumption of **orthodox science** is very, very wrong!*

Human consciousness, properly applied, isa significant thermodynamic variable in the conduct of orthodox experiments in the study of nature.

The description of Professor Tiller's 2007 book, *'Phychoenergetic Science: A Second Copernican Revolution,'* describes how modifying future probability with intent is not a *'woo-woo'* concept, but instead **a fundamental aspect of our reality**:

*The fourth book in Dr. Tiller s remarkable psychoenergetic science series is an integrator of the first three in much simpler language and with practically no mathematical equations. It has been written for the intellectual level of an undergraduate college student. Here, he shows why and how both (1) today s quantum mechanics must be expanded to include human consciousness as a significant experimental variable in today s physics and (2) expansion of our reference frame for viewing nature s manifold expressions in domains other than spacetime are required by us to seriously integrate human consciousness into a new paradigm. **His earlier work has revealed a second, unique level of physical reality which can be integrated with the first, our normal*** *electric atom/molecule level, via the proper use of human consciousness to condition normal space to a higher electromagnetic symmetry state. In this coupled system, <u>human intentions can significantly modulate material properties as detected instrumentally.</u> The newer work reveals a detector system that provides continuous measurement of conditioned spaces to show a quantitative measure of the excess energy of such a space compared to our normal reality. In addition, this work has shown that the human acupuncture meridian/chakra system is at this higher symmetry state in an overall body which is not. Thus, directed and focused intentions by individual humans diligently working on themselves can transform them into higher states of beingness.* Finally, in Chapter 8, Dr. Tiller shows us why these psychoenergetic science applications will usher into our world revolutionary changes of at least Copernican-scale magnitude!

The Database

"I see the Past, Present & Future existing all at once before me." –
William Blake (English Poet; 1757 – 1827)

In a virtual-reality video game, data from the past is stored and used to calculate the present; presenting the player with choices based upon past history.

Tom Campbell maintains that the same holds true in our virtual-reality simulation. The database housing our virtual reality simulation, however, appears much more robust than any video games which have thus far been created.

The *life database*, also known as the *'Akashic Records'*, houses not just information regarding the actualized past, but also the non-actualized past, according to Campbell.

The actualized past determines the present, with all probable future outcomes housed in the database as well.

An article posted on *Edgar Cayce's Association for Research and Enlightenment* (*edgarcayce.org*) outlines the *life database*, which is consistent with Campbell's description:

*The Akashic Records, or "**The Book of Life**," can be equaled to the*
***universe's super-computer system**. It is this system that acts as the*
*central storehouse of **all information** for every individual who has ever*
lived upon the earth. More than just a reservoir of events, the Akashic
*Records contain **every deed, word, feeling, thought, and intent that has**
ever occurred at any time in the history of the world. Much more than*
simply a memory storehouse, however, these Akashic Records are
***interactive** in that they have a tremendous influence upon our everyday*
lives, our relationships, our feelings and belief systems, and the potential
realities we draw toward us.

When we practice remote viewing, research past lives, or attempt to
foresee the *probabilistic* future, we are essentially tapping into *the
database*.

Daryl Bem, Professor Emeritus at *Cornell University*, claims that this *psi*
phenomenon can be demonstrated in a scientific setting.

Bem authored a 2011 paper in the *Journal of Personality and Social
Psychology* titled *'Feeling the Future: Experimental Evidence for
Anomalous: Retroactive Influences on Cognition and Affect'*
documenting his findings.

A 2010 article on *The Cornell Daily Sun* (*cornellsun.com*) titled *'Psychic
Precognition May Exist, Cornell Study Finds'* outlines Bem's *controversial*
findings:

*Through nine experiments at the University involving more than 1,000
students, Bem confirmed his hypotheses in all but one of the
experiments. This signified that evidence of psi exists, since "**the odds
against the possibility that the combined results are merely chance
coincidences or statistical flukes are about 74 billion to 1**," according to
Bem. In his first experiment, Bem explored the effects of erotic stimuli on
perceiving the future. After being shown an image, one hundred Cornell
students — 50 male and 50 female — were each shown pictures of two
curtained screens on computer monitors, one covering a blank wall, the*

*other covering the image. Many but not all of the pictures behind the curtains were erotic images, such as those of "couples engaged in nonviolent but explicit consensual sexual acts," according to Bem's paper. Each participant was to click on the curtain which he or she thought had the picture behind it.Bem hypothesized that 50 percent of those who were shown erotic stimuli would identify the correct curtain, and that those shown erotic pictures would have a higher "hit rate" — the number of times that the correct curtain was identified — than participants that were shown non-erotic pictures. In the 100 sessions, the hit rate for those shown erotic stimuli was 53.1 percent, while the 49.8 percent hit rate of those shown non-erotic pictures did not deviate from chance. This shows that on average, given that the erotic image shown to the participant made a considerable impression, **that participant's ability to foresee the future is statistically higher than chance**, according to Bem. "The remarkable finding [we made] is that **their physiological responses are observed to occur about 2-3 seconds prior to the appearance of the picture, even before the computer has decided whether to present a non-arousing or an arousing picture**," Bem said.The results of the other eight experiments, which were conducted using different types of stimuli, were similar to those of the first.*

The conclusion would not be considered 'proof', but offers yet another mainstream data-point which *only* makes logical sense in a virtual reality.

'Experience Packets'

"As a man, casting off worn out garments taketh new ones, so the dweller in the body, entereth into ones that are new." — Epictetus (Ancient Greek Philosopher)

When an avatar dies, it is **no longer a physical player in this virtual-reality simulation.**

In a virtual-reality game, the player dies, but the 'ghost in the machine', or the consciousness that played the character, **persists.**

Unlike *The Sims*, where a player can die and return as the exact same avatar, players in this *game* don't appear to have that option.

Once the avatar dies, **it is no longer in the game as that character** and later '*respawns*' as a totally different avatar, facing new challenges with different constraints, while retaining their cumulative '*quality of consciousness*'.

In gaming, the process of maintaining certain aspects of '*being*' through multiple lifetimes is known as the *'new game plus'* feature.

Tom Campbell describes each *physical-matter reality* lifetime as an **'experience packet'** – the current life experience that a *'free will awareness unit'* is having.

When an avatar dies, the information is absorbed into the *'individuated unit of consciousness'*, or the *'oversoul'*, and incorporated into the next *'experience packet'*, in Campbell's model.

Our *evolving* consciousness, operating in many virtual realities, has likely experienced hundreds or thousands of *'experience packets'*, and is logically **likely to experience thousands more**.

The prospect of living multiple lives, or *reincarnation*, is often seen as *new age* hocus-pocus, though a surprising percentage of people inherently understand that this **physical-matter reality is not fundamental.**

*"It is the secret of the world that all things subsist and do not die, **but only retire a little from sight and afterward return again**."* – Ralph Waldo Emerson (1803-1882; American Author)

A 2017 *huffingtonpost.com* article titled *'Spooky Number Of Americans Believe In Ghosts'* demonstrates that we inherently understand that **death is not final**:

*Of the 1,000 adults interviewed Dec. 17-18, the HuffPost/YouGov poll revealed 45 percent believe in ghosts, or that the spirits of dead people can come back in certain places and situations. When asked if they believe there's a life after death, **64 percent responded Yes**. While 59 percent of adults don't believe they've ever actually seen a ghost, 43*

*percent also don't think that ghosts or spirits can harm or interact with
living people.*

*The results aren't far off from previous polls, including a CBS News 2009
study, which showed that "nearly half of Americans say they believe in
ghosts, or that the dead can return in certain places and situations."
That poll also revealed that **78 percent of Americans believe in life after
death**.*

Reincarnation is fundamental within virtual realities. If our spirit, soul,
or consciousness, lives on after our avatar dies, then logically **we have
had past avatars as well**.

During each *'experience packet'*, we get tangled up in belief patterns
and dogmas which would not be useful to our future avatars. Our
'quality of consciousness', as Tom Campbell refers to it, **is immortal**,
while our belief-system gets *deleted, or wiped clean,* between physical
lives.

Each new life presents new challenges and opportunities, while our past
life experiences are retained within the database. Most don't knowingly
have any recollection of past lives, though some do.

A 2014 article on *psychologytoday.com* titled *'Children Who Seemingly
Remember Past Lives: Why might some children recount apparent past
life memories with such vividness?'* sheds light on this *impossible*
phenomenon:

*The ultimate 'truth is stranger than fiction' accounts are to be found
in Return to Life: Extraordinary Cases of Children Who Remember Past
Lives, a book published last year by Jim Tucker, a psychiatry professor at
the University of Virginia. Tucker follows in the footsteps of the late Ian
Stevenson, who for decades scrupulously investigated cases in which
young children around the world spontaneously volunteered – **in great
detail – recollections that seemed to be about someone else's life**.
Much of the time, the person being spoken of had died violently or*

unnaturally. *(In a prior post, I referenced one such instance, where a two-and-a-half-year old girl became distraught over her inability to find 'her' children and described 'her' having lost her life in a road accident.)* **Between them, Stevenson and Tucker have compiled more than 2,500 cases and 70% of them fit this pattern**.

It is also important to note that these '*past life*' memories can have a profound effect on our current life-experience (the article continues):

It's nearly impossible to conceive how children so young should have such vivid 'memories' or how they (or anyone connected with them, for that matter) could have known anything about such obscure figures from the past, whether it be Martin Martyn or "Little Man" James Huston. Nor do such children appear to be abused or suffering from any trauma connected with their current life. Furthermore, the families in these cases are firmly believing Christians for whom the concept of reincarnation is foreign. The parents, besides being vexed in the extreme, are inevitably reluctant to have their children's cases publicized for fear of being mocked.

These types of memories typically fade, by the way, around six years of age, according to Tucker. The kids involved usually express a desire as well to fully embrace the life they're in now.

However, the degree to which these children show heightened emotion in recounting these apparent memories is a tipoff, to me, that something truly significant is going on. **A boy like James Leininger shows all the hallmarks of PTSD at age two; why should he? We can get a sense for the answer by realizing how fear – that most elemental of feelings – puts our entire being on red alert.** *The pupils dilate, muscles are tensed, and respiration is increased as the body prepares to fight, flee, or freeze. Meanwhile, the hypothalamic-pituitary-adrenal (HPA) axis springs into action by releasing a cascade of hormones that serve to marshal bodily energy. If we are indeed in mortal peril, our entire bodymind tenses like a spring ready to snap. Our senses are honed to a fine edge: we notice every detail that could affect our existence.*

166

But consider what would ensue if all that energy had no outlet – if, because of a sudden accident or foul play, someone could neither fight nor flee but were trapped in freeze mode? We know that rats that are given even a mild shock somehow transfer the fear associated with the particular stimulus on to their pups, and even to their pups' pups. **Could there be a mechanism, somewhere between life and death, where memories associated with the struggling person's circumstances are preserved***? It would be akin to the echoes, preserved down the eons, of the Big Bang observable through faint but distinct background radiation. Except in the cases we are considering, the intensity of the person's feelings –* **his or her life energy, self-awareness and being – might somehow be captured in a fusion of space and time. This 'imprint' might become available for another, nascent life form – not "his" or "her" memories (as in reincarnation) but a transmutation just the same.**

Simulation _Speculation_

Similar to a player living within _The Sims_, we have no way to examine the computer powering our reality, as we can only interact with its _downstream_ effects.

Inside our _physical-matter_ simulation, learning the origin of the force behind consciousness, as well as its innermost workings, is purely speculation.

The question of how something can be created from nothing is a paradox with no definitive answer from our vantage-point, but our desire to understand persists nonetheless.

In a 1988 article on _theatlantic.com_ profiling Edward Fredkin – pioneer in the field of _digital physics_ - titled _'Did the Universe Just Happen'_, the concept of _cellular automata_ – or the self-replicating code seemingly underlying _physical-matter reality_ – is detailed:

The prime mover of everything, the single principle that governs the universe, lies somewhere within a **class of computer programs known as cellular automata**, according to Fredkin.

The cellular automaton was invented in the early 1950s by John von Neumann, one of the architects of computer science and a seminal thinker in several other fields. Von Neumann (who was stimulated in this and other inquiries by the ideas of the mathematician Stanislaw Ulam) **saw cellular automata as a way to study reproduction abstractly, but the word cellular is not meant biologically when used in this context. It refers, rather, to adjacent spaces—cells—that together form a pattern.**

These days the cells typically appear on a computer screen, though von Neumann, lacking this convenience, rendered them on paper.

In some respects cellular automata resemble those splendid graphic displays produced by patriotic masses in authoritarian societies and by avid football fans at American universities. Holding up large colored cards on cue, they can collectively generate a portrait of, say, Lenin, Mao Zedong, or a University of Southern California Trojan. More impressive still, one portrait can fade out and another crystallize in no time at all. **Again and again one frozen frame melts into another It is a spectacular feat of precision and planning.**

But suppose there were no planning. Suppose that instead of arranging a succession of cards to display, everyone learned a single rule for repeatedly determining which card was called for next. This rule might assume any of a number of forms. For example, in a crowd where all cards were either blue or white, each card holder could be instructed to look at his own card and the cards of his four nearest neighbors—to his front, back, left, and right—and do what the majority did during the last frame. (This five-cell group is known as the von Neumann neighborhood.) Alternatively, each card holder could be instructed to do the opposite of what the majority did. In either event the result would be a series not of predetermined portraits but of **more abstract, unpredicted patterns**. *If, by prior agreement, we began with a USC Trojan, its white face might dissolve into a sea of blue, as whitecaps drifted aimlessly across the stadium. Conversely, an ocean of randomness could yield islands of structure—not a Trojan, perhaps, but at least something that didn't look entirely accidental.* **It all depends on the original pattern of cells and the rule used to transform it incrementally.**

This leaves room for abundant variety. *There are many ways to define a neighborhood, and for any given neighborhood there are* **many**

169

possible rules, most of them more complicated than blind conformity or implacable nonconformity. Each cell may, for instance, not only count cells in the vicinity but also pay attention to which particular cells are doing what. All told**, the number of possible rules is an exponential function of the number of cells in the neighborhoo**d; the von Neumann neighborhood alone has 2^{32}, or around 4 billion, possible rules, and the nine-cell neighborhood that results from adding corner cells offers 2^{512}, or roughly 1 with 154 zeros after it, possibilities. But whatever neighborhoods, and whatever rules, are programmed into a computer, two things are always true of cellular automata: **all cells use the same rule to determine future behavior by reference to the past behavior of neighbors, and all cells obey the rule simultaneously, time after time.**

In the late 1950s, shortly after becoming acquainted with cellular automata, Fredkin began playing around with rules, selecting the powerful and interesting and discarding the weak and bland. He found, for example, that any rule requiring **all four of a cell's immediate neighbors to be lit up in order for the cell itself to be lit up at the next moment** would not provide sustained entertainment; a single "off" cell would proliferate until darkness covered the computer screen. **But equally simple rules could create great complexity.** The first such rule discovered by Fredkin dictated that a cell be on if an odd number of cells in its von Neumann neighborhood had been on, and off otherwise. After "seeding" a good, powerful rule with an irregular landscape of off and on cells, Fredkin could watch **rich patterns bloom, some freezing upon maturity, some eventually dissipating, others locking into a cycle of growth and decay**. A colleague, after watching one of Fredkin's rules in action, suggested that he sell the program to a designer of Persian rugs.

Today new **cellular-automaton rules are formulated and tested by the "information-mechanics group" founded by Fredkin at MIT's computer-science laboratory**. The core of the group is an international duo of physicists, Tommaso Toffoli, of Italy, and Norman Margolus, of

170

Canada. They differ in the degree to which they take Fredkin's theory of physics seriously, but both agree with him that there is value in exploring the **relationship between computation and physics,** *and they have spent much time using* **cellular automata to simulate physical processes**. *In the basement of the computer-science laboratory is the CAM—the cellular automaton machine, designed by Toffoli and Margolus partly for that purpose. Its screen has 65,536 cells, each of which can assume any of four colors and can change color sixty times a second.*

The CAM is an engrossing, potentially mesmerizing machine. Its four colors—the three primaries and black—intermix rapidly and intricately enough to form subtly shifting hues of almost any gradation; **pretty waves of deep blue or red ebb and flow with fine fluidity and sometimes with rhythm, playing on the edge between chaos and order.**

Guided by the right rule, the CAM **can do a respectable imitation of pond water rippling outward circularly in deference to a descending pebble, or of bubbles forming at the bottom of a pot of boiling water, or of a snowflake blossoming from a seed of ice: step by step, a single "ice crystal" in the center of the screen unfolds into a full-fledged flake, a six-edged sheet of ice riddled symmetrically with dark pockets of mist.** *(It is easy to see how a cellular automaton can capture the principles thought to govern the growth of a snowflake: regions of vapor that find themselves in the vicinity of a budding snowflake freeze— unless so nearly enveloped by ice crystals that they cannot discharge enough heat to freeze.)*

These exercises are fun to watch, and they give one a sense of the cellular automaton's power, but Fredkin is not particularly interested in them. After all, a snowflake is not, at the visible level, literally a cellular automaton; an ice crystal is not a single, indivisible bit of information, like the cell that portrays it. Fredkin believes that **automata will more faithfully mirror reality as they are applied to its more fundamental levels and the rules needed to model the motion of molecules, atoms, electrons, and quarks are uncovered.** *And he believes that at the most fundamental level (whatever that turns out to be)* <u>**the automaton will describe the physical world with perfect precision, because at that level the universe is a cellular automaton, in three dimensions—a crystalline lattice of interacting logic units, each one "deciding" zillions of point in time. The information thus produced, Fredkin says, is the fabric of reality, the stuff of which matter and energy are made. An electron, in Fredkin's universe, is nothing more than a pattern of information, and an orbiting electron is nothing more than that pattern moving.**</u> *Indeed, even this motion is in some sense illusory: the bits of information that constitute the pattern never move, any more than football fans would change places to slide a USC Trojan four seats to the left. Each bit stays put and confines its activity to blinking on and off. "You see, I don't believe that there are objects like electrons and photons, and things which are themselves and nothing else," Fredkin says. What I believe is that there's an information process, and the bits, when they're in certain configurations, behave like the thing we call the electron, or the hydrogen atom, or whatever."*

In The Beginning...

1 In the beginning God created the heaven and the earth.

2 And the earth was without form, and void; and darkness was upon the face of the deep. And the Spirit of God moved upon the face of the waters.

3 And God said, Let there be light: and there was light.

-*Genesis 1-3*; King James Bible Version (KJV)

The story of *Genesis* describes how '*God*' created the universe.

Inside a virtual-reality simulation, the beginning of time would be likened to a computer booting-up; Thomas Campbell refers to this idea as the '*digital big bang*'.

A creation story *similar* to *Genesis* is the Sumerian *Enuma Elish*, which is the creation story of the earliest *officially documented* civilization. Various clay tablets describing the event have been recovered, and the most commonly referenced version is that of the Babylonians, which is thought to have been etched around 1,800 B.C.

California State University at Northridge, at *CSUN.edu*, provides a description of the Babylonian *Enuma Elish*:

*The Enuma Elish (which are the first two words of the epic and mean simply "When on high") is the creation myth of ancient Mesopotamia. This is the Babylonian **version of a much older Sumerian myth** and originally the chief figure of the myth was Enlil, the Sumerian storm god. When Babylon conquered the rest of Mesopotamia and established the Old Babylonian Empire around 1800 BCE, it became necessary to explain how the local god of Babylon, Marduk, had now become supreme among the gods. Therefore, the older Sumerian myth of creation was retold and Marduk was substituted for Enlil.*

The piece continues to provide a translation of the text:

When on high the heaven had not been named,1

Firm ground below had not been called by name,

Naught but primordial Apsu, their begetter,

(And) Mummu2 Tiamat, she who bore them all,

Their waters commingling as a single body,3

No reed but had been matted, no marsh land had appeared,2

When no gods whatever had been brought into being,

Un-named, their destinies yet undermined—

Then it was that the gods were emerged from within them.

The *Enuma Elish* goes on to describe how physical *"Gods"* spontaneously emerged, assuming leadership roles within a seemingly already-advanced civilization. This methodology is consistent with *NPCs*, or *non-player characters*, inserted within virtual-reality simulations to assume certain roles and responsibilities.

The Golden Age

(*'**The Golden Age**' by Lucas Cranach of Elder*)

According to Greek mythology, there were five successive '*Ages of Man*'; the first is known as '*The Golden Age*'.

Greek poet *Hesiod*, in a late 6th century B.C. writing titled '*Works and Days*', describes the *mythical* Golden Age:

[Men] lived like gods without sorrow of heart, remote and free from toil and grief: *miserable age rested not on them; but with **legs and arms never failing they made merry with feasting** beyond the reach of all devils. When they died, it was as though they were overcome with sleep, and **they had all good things; <u>for the fruitful earth unforced bare them fruit abundantly and without stint. They dwelt in ease and peace.</u>***

The Golden Age is known for being a time when all of life's necessities were abundant, requiring very little struggle or conflict.

This point is alluded to in the 1999 movie '*The Matrix*', as Agent Smith describes the problems of the first *simulation* to Neo:

Did you know that **the first Matrix was designed to be a perfect human world? Where none suffered, where everyone would be happy. <u>It was a disaster. No one would accept the program</u>**. *Entire crops were lost. Some believed we lacked the programming language to describe your perfect world. But I believe that, as a species, human beings define their reality through suffering and misery. The perfect world was a dream that your primitive cerebrum kept trying to wake up from. Which is why* **the Matrix was redesigned** *to this: the peak of your civilization.*

If a prior simulation was not meeting its *entropy-reduction* mandate, and if the players didn't truly accept the authenticity of the game, it would've had to be *re-booted*.

Great Flood(s)

(Image description from Wikipedia: *"The Deluge", frontispiece to Gustave Doré's illustrated edition of the Bible. Based on the story of Noah's Ark, this shows humans and a tiger doomed by the flood futilely attempting to save their children and cubs*)

If a virtual-reality simulation is failing to meet its entropy-reduction requirement, engulfing the virtual reality in a massive flood would serve to reset the scenario and allow a refined, or *updated*, program to run.

The idea that flash floods previously wiped-out humanity is a fundamental concept within documented history. *Genesis 6:17* of the *King James Bible* describes the '*Great Flood*':

*And, behold, I, even I, do bring a flood of waters upon the earth, **to destroy all flesh**, wherein is the breath of life, from under heaven; and **every thing that is in the earth shall die.***

Anyone who witnessed and survived such events, or saw the aftermath, would surely question how an all-loving '*God*' could do such a thing, unaware that a *simulation-reset* was potentially required to prevent increasing entropy and the eventual dissolution of *'the larger consciousness system'*.

The Reality Program

All the world's a stage,

And all the men and women merely players;

They have their exits and their entrances.

- William Shakespeare (1564 – 1616)

If there were prior simulation resets, with entire reality paradigms wiped-out and *rebooted*, certain historical anomalies would be easily explainable.

Author Graham Hancock, researcher of ancient cultural anomalies, demonstrates that accepted mainstream explanations regarding ancient civilizations don't make logical sense.

In his 2012 book '*Fingerprints of the Gods: The Evidence of Earth's Lost Civilization*', Hancock describes the paradox:

*Ancient Egypt, like that of the Olmecs (Bolivia), **emerged all at once and fully formed**. Indeed, the period of transition from primitive to advanced society appears to have been so short that it makes no kind of historical* *sense. Technological skills that should have taken hundreds or even thousands of years to evolve were* **brought into use almost overnight-- and with no apparent antecedents whatever**. *For example, remains from the pre-dynastic period around 3500 BC show no trace of writing. Soon after that date, quite suddenly and inexplicably, the hieroglyphs familiar from so many of the ruins of Ancient Egypt begin to appear in a complete and perfect state. Far from being mere pictures of objects or actions, this written language was complex and structured at the outset, with signs that represented sounds only and a detailed system of numerical symbols. Even the very earliest hieroglyphs were stylized and conventionalized; and it is clear that an advanced cursive script was it common usage by the dawn of the First Dynasty.*

The *Pyramids of Egypt* highlight the fact that ancient engineering appears more advanced than our current capabilities.

In his 1998 book titled '*The Giza Power Plant: Technologies of Ancient Egypt*', author Christopher Dunn demonstrates how the *Great Pyramid of Giza* would be a massive – *if not impossible* - undertaking, even by today's standards:

It goes without saying that if we were to build a Great Pyramid today, we would need a lot of patience. In preparation for his book **5/5/2000 Ice: The Ultimate Disaster**, *Richard Noone asked Merle Booker, technical director of the Indiana Limestone Institute of America, to prepare a time study of what it would take to quarry, fabricate, and ship enough limestone to duplicate the Great Pyramid. Using the most modern quarrying equipment available for cutting, lifting, and transporting the stone, Booker estimated that the present-day Indiana limestone industry would need to triple its output, and it would take the entire industry, which as I have said includes* **thirty-three quarries, twenty-seven years to fill the order for 131,467,940 cubic feet of stone. These estimates were based on the assumption that production would proceed without problems. Then we would be faced with the task of putting the limestone blocks in place.**

180

It is important to note that the preceding estimate is only in regards to the *Great Pyramid of Giza*, and not the other nearby pyramids, or the *Sphinx*.

Christopher Dunn continues to demonstrate the *absurdity* of our historical assumptions surrounding ancient Egypt:

For those who may still believe in the "official" chronology of the historical development of metals, **identifying copper as the metal the ancient Egyptians used for cutting granite is like saying that aluminum could be cut using a chisel fashioned out of butter.**

Religion

*"**We live in illusion and the appearance of things**. There is a reality. We are that reality. When you understand this, you see that you are nothing, and being nothing, you are everything. That is all."* — Gautama Buddha (founder of Buddhism; circa 563 B.C. to 483 B.C.)

The idea that we are part of something larger and ultimately interconnected is not a new, or solely '*new-age*', concept. Nikola Tesla describes how interconnectedness is **ingrained within all of humanity**:

*For ages this idea has been proclaimed in the consummately wise teachings of religion, probably not alone as a means of insuring peace and harmony among men, **but as a deeply founded truth**. The Buddhist expresses it in one way, the Christian in another, but both say the same:* **We are all one.**

Tom Campbell, in '*My Big TOE: Awakening*', explains how most religions were founded on the same guiding principles:

All spiritual paths converge on the same absolute truths by means of reducing ego and fear , which are the primary generators of confusion and divisiveness .

'*The larger consciousness system*', holding all of the attributes of '*God*', is largely subjective, and when we try to make it objective – or absolute – conflicts arise.

Quantum physics and the study of consciousness demonstrate that our physical world is virtual, powered outside of the physical world.

This information shouldn't serve as another religious doctrine, but may instead be viewed as a scientifically demonstrated phenomenon *worthy* of our attention.

Simulation Pontification

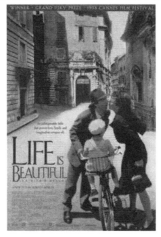

"Our lives are but specks of dust falling through the fingers of time. Like sands of the hourglass, so are the days of our lives." - Greek Philosopher Socrates

Seconds turn to minutes; minutes turn to hours; days turn to months; months turn to years; years turn to *lifetimes*.

We ponder how *'time flies'* as we struggle through life, often feeling like the deck is stacked against us; like we are *doomed to fail* from the outset.

It is easy to dwell on the tedium and *chaos* of the daily grind, but shifting our gaze inward is the key to self-improvement, and the only way out of the *mental-maze* holding many of us captive.

'The LCS Loves You'

"And we have known and believed the love that God hath to us. God is love; and he that dwelleth in love dwelleth in God, and God in him." - King James Bible: **1 John 4:16**

Tom Campbell describes that *'the larger consciousness system'* has a vested interest in our success; expressing unconditional *digital-love* for its children:

*The bottom line is that the larger consciousness system is **designed and constructed to support your personal growth in every and any way that could possibly be effective for you. It will not help you experience things that are likely to increase your entropy -- you do enough of that yourself.***

The difference between happiness and misery is determined by how we *process data*, regardless of the data itself.

Ann Frank, secretly living inside occupied territory for two years beginning at the age of twelve, demonstrates the power of *'the larger consciousness system'* in her published diary entries titled *'The Diary of a Young Girl'*:

*People who have a religion should be glad, for not everyone has the gift of believing in heavenly things. **You don't necessarily even have to be afraid of punishment after death;** purgatory, hell, and heaven are things that a lot of people can't accept, but still a religion, it doesn't matter which, keeps a person on the right path. **It isn't the fear of God but <u>the upholding of one's own honor and conscience</u>**. How noble and good everyone could be if, every evening before falling asleep, they were to recall to their minds the events of the while day and consider exactly* *what has been good and bad. Then, without realizing it you* **try to improve yourself at the start of each new day***; of course, you achieve quite a lot in the course of time. Anyone can do this, it costs nothing and is certainly very helpful. Whoever doesn't know it must learn and find by experience that: "A quiet conscience mades one strong!*

Get in the Game

*"I've made the most important discovery of my life. **It's only in the mysterious equation of love that any logical reasons can be found.** I'm only here tonight because of you. You're the only reason I am...you're all my reasons."* – John Nash (1994 Nobel Prize Winner)

Our *physical-matter virtual reality* is wrought with sorrow and tragedy, while also exuding warmth and kindness.

Our role within this virtual reality is to improve ourselves by reducing our fear and ego, in-turn improving the '*system*', **which we all belong to**, and which **loves us unconditionally**.

*"The gift of mental power comes from God, Divine Being, and if we concentrate our minds on that truth, **we become in tune with this great power**."* – Nikola Tesla

In our day-to-day lives, we are either working to improve, or evolve, or we are *de-evolving*. *Stasis* – or remaining the same – is not a long-term option.

Many - if not most - of our lives are filled with regret.

Bronnie Ware, author of several books including '*The Top Five Regrets of the Dying: A Life Transformed by the Dearly Departing*', spent years with terminally ill patients. In an article on *bronnieware.com* titled '*Regrets of the Dying*,' Ware outlines the regrets most of us *will* come to harbor:

1. I wish I'd had **the courage** to live a life true to myself, not the life others expected of me.

*This was the most common regret of all. When people realise that their life is almost over and look back clearly on it, it is easy to see how many dreams have gone unfulfilled. Most people had not honoured even a half of their dreams and had to die knowing that it was **due to choices they had made, or not made.***

*It is very important to try and honour at least some of your dreams along the way. From the moment that you lose your health, it is too late. **Health brings a freedom very few realise, until they no longer have it.***

2. I wish I hadn't worked so hard.

*This came from **every** male patient that I nursed. They missed their children's youth and their partner's companionship. Women also spoke of this regret. But as most were from an older generation, many of the female patients had not been breadwinners. All of the men I nursed deeply regretted spending so much of their lives on the treadmill of a work existence.*

By simplifying your lifestyle and making conscious choices along the way, it is possible to not need the income that you think you do. And by creating more space in your life, you become happier and more open to new opportunities, ones more suited to your new lifestyle.

3. I wish I'd had the **courage** to express my feelings.

Many people suppressed their feelings in order to keep peace with others. As a result, they settled for a mediocre existence and never became who they were truly capable of becoming. Many developed illnesses relating to the bitterness and resentment they carried as a result.

187

We cannot control the reactions of others. However, although people may initially react when you change the way you are by speaking honestly, in the end it raises the relationship to a whole new and healthier level. Either that or it releases the unhealthy relationship from your life. Either way, you win.

4. I wish I had stayed in touch with my friends.

Often they would not truly realise the full benefits of old friends until their dying weeks and it was not always possible to track them down. Many had become so caught up in their own lives that they had let golden friendships slip by over the years. There were many deep regrets about not giving friendships the time and effort that they deserved. Everyone misses their friends when they are dying.

*It is common for anyone in a busy lifestyle to let friendships slip. But when you are faced with your approaching death, the physical details of life fall away. People do want to get their financial affairs in order if possible. But it is not money or status that holds the true importance for them. They want to get things in order more for the benefit of those they love. Usually though, they are too ill and weary to ever manage this task. It all comes down to love and relationships in the end. **That is all that remains in the final weeks, <u>love and relationships.</u>***

*5. I wish that I had **let myself be happier**.*

*This is a surprisingly common one. Many did not realise until the end that **<u>happiness is a choice</u>**. **<u>They had stayed stuck in old patterns and habits. The so-called 'comfort' of familiarity overflowed into their emotions, as well as their physical lives. Fear of change had them pretending to others, and to their selves, that they were content. When deep within, they longed to laugh properly and have silliness in their life again.</u>***

<u>When you are on your deathbed, what others think of you is a long way from your mind. How wonderful to be able to let go and smile</u>

188

again, long before you are dying.

Life is a choice. It is YOUR life. Choose consciously, choose wisely, choose honestly. Choose happiness.

Tom Campbell's *Big Theory of Everything* demonstrates that it doesn't matter where we have been, but where we are going that counts.

"To err is human; to forgive, divine" - Alexander Pope (English poet; 1688–1744)

Once we **choose** to stop growing, our current *'experience packet'* is essentially over. When we stop trying to improve ourselves, and therefore *'the larger consciousness system'*, *'the system'* logically ceases investing its resources in us.

The *quality of our consciousness* is cumulative – **spanning lifetimes**. By choosing to stop growing, we only delay our inevitable journey towards improvement.

Our current experiences, as serious or permanent as they may seem, *will eventually fade away.*

16th US President Abraham Lincoln (1809-1865) reminded us of the *impermanence* of our lives:

It is said an Eastern monarch once charged his wise men to invent him a sentence to be ever in view, and which should be **true and appropriate in all times and situations***. They presented him the words, "**And this too, shall pass away***." How much it expresses!* **How chastening in the hour of pride! How consoling in the depths of affliction!**

Understanding that our *physical-matter reality* is virtual, and that we indeed have a purpose, may provide the impetus to improve ourselves and work towards *'becoming love'*, or more practically reducing fear and ego.

Understanding that our *physical-matter virtual reality* is a *labyrinth,* designed to challenge us and force us to make decisions, requires a paradigm-shift of epic proportions.

Stereotypes, biases, and hatred take on a different meaning when we realize that we are all essentially *peas in a pod,* assuming different roles in different lifetimes.

An American soldier killed in the Vietnam War could be *reborn* as a Vietnamese girl; a mass-murdering dictator could be *reborn* as a Chinese farmer; the possibilities and irony are endless in our *physical-matter virtual reality.*

Improvement is not an easy thing to do, but de-evolving, and allowing fear to control us, is arguably much worse.

Getting acquainted with our *being level* and '*living gracefully with uncertainty*', as Tom Campbell describes, opens the door to a much larger, and more joyous, life experience.

We are made of information, and information surrounds us. The quicker this information reaches the mainstream, the quicker our shared *gaming-experience* can be drastically changed.

Whether it changes for the better, or for the worse, is another matter...

The choice is ours.

*"What we now want is closer contact and better understanding between individuals and communities all over the earth, and the elimination of egoism and pride which is always prone to plunge the world into primeval barbarism and strife... **Peace can only come as a natural consequence of universal enlightenment**.*" – Nikola Tesla

Afterward

Thank you for reading this book. This information has impacted me profoundly, and my sincerest hope is that you find some of this information useful, relevant, and applicable to improving your/our reality.

If you do find this information helpful and pertinent to your life, I would humbly ask for a review on amazon. Feedback is very limited through this medium, and only a very small percentage of readers comment. I ask in the hopes that it helps to spread this information, so that this *information can be applied* to our reality sooner rather than later.

I have never met, nor have any affiliation with, Tom Campbell, and I feel that one day his work will be seen – on a much-larger scale - as paradigm-shifting.

Tom Campbell has designed quantum physics experiments, **which can be performed with materials available at any established physics laboratory**, which take the double-slit experiments further, and will definitively demonstrate that physical-matter reality is secondary to a much larger reality.

Information on the experiments, as well as hundreds of hours of valuable information, are available on Tom Campbell's *Youtube* channel, or his website, *my-big-toe.com*.

My other writings and assorted information, which tend to take a deep-dive into many of the anomalies within our *physical-matter reality*, are available on my website, *casperstith.com*, and available for direct purchase on *amazon.com*.

Casper Stith

Printed in Great Britain
by Amazon

68533317R00113